NEW DIRECTIONS FOR MENTAL h _ _ _

H. Richard Lamb, *University of Southern California*
EDITOR-IN-CHIEF

Using Trauma Theory to Design Service Systems

Maxine Harris
Community Connections

Roger D. Fallot
Community Connections

EDITORS

Number 89, Spring 2001

JOSSEY-BASS
San Francisco

Using Trauma Theory to Design Service Systems
Maxine Harris, Roger D. Fallot (eds.)
New Directions for Mental Health Services, no. 89
H. Richard Lamb, Editor-in-Chief

Microfilm copies of issues and articles are available in 16mm and 35mm, as well as microfiche in 105mm, through University Microfilms Inc., 300 North Zeeb Road, Ann Arbor, Michigan 48106–1346.

ISSN 0193–9416   ISBN 0–7879–1438-X

NEW DIRECTIONS FOR MENTAL HEALTH SERVICES is part of The Jossey-Bass Psychology Series and is published quarterly by Jossey-Bass Inc., Publishers, 350 Sansome Street, San Francisco, California 94104-1342.

SUBSCRIPTIONS cost $66.00 for individuals and $121.00 for institutions, agencies, and libraries.

EDITORIAL CORRESPONDENCE should be sent to the Editor-in-Chief, H. Richard Lamb, University of Southern California, Department of Psychiatry, Graduate Hall, 1937 Hospital Place, Los Angeles, California 90033–1071.

Cover photograph by Wernher Krutein/PHOTOVAULT ©1990.

Jossey-Bass Web address: www.josseybass.com

CONTENTS

EDITORS' NOTES   1
Maxine Harris, Roger D. Fallot

1. Envisioning a Trauma-Informed Service System: 3
A Vital Paradigm Shift
Maxine Harris, Roger D. Fallot
All components of the service system need to be reconsidered and eval-
uated in the light of a basic understanding of the role that violence plays
in the lives of people seeking mental health and addictions services.

2. A Trauma-Informed Approach to Screening and Assessment   23
Roger D. Fallot, Maxine Harris
The widespread underreporting and underrecognition of sexual and
physical abuse pose special challenges for designing trauma-informed
screening and assessment procedures.

3. Trauma-Informed Inpatient Services   33
Maxine Harris, Roger D. Fallot
Community alternatives to inpatient treatment for trauma survivors are
considered along with suggestions for modifying inpatient practices.

4. Trauma-Informed Approaches to Housing   47
Richard R. Bebout
This chapter describes the measures that residential programs might
want to consider in order to respect the needs and vulnerabilities of
trauma survivors.

5. Designing Trauma-Informed Addictions Services   57
Maxine Harris, Roger D. Fallot
Substance abuse and its relationship to violence and victimization are
considered, along with suggestions for designing services that accommodate the needs of trauma survivors.

6. Trauma-Informed Services and Case Management   75
David W. Freeman
This chapter compares a traditional case management approach to one
that operates from a strengths-based, consumer-focused orientation.

7. Defining the Role of Consumer-Survivors   83
in Trauma-Informed Systems
Laura Prescott
The consumer-survivor's active participation in all phases of service
development and delivery is a vital component of a trauma-informed
approach to service delivery.

8. Care of the Clinician   91
Ellen Arledge, Rebecca Wolfson
Trauma has an impact not only on those who have been directly vic-
timized; it also affects those who deliver services.

INDEX   99

EDITORS' NOTES

Practitioners who deliver mental health, addictions, case management, and residential services to consumers in a variety of community and hospital settings are becoming increasingly aware that they are encountering a very large number of men and women who are survivors of sexual and physical abuse. Although an abuse history is rarely the immediate precipitant to a consumer's decision to seek services, it is a factor that informs and complicates the treatment experience for both the consumer and the provider. An understanding of trauma, its sequelae, and the impact that it has in shaping a consumer's response to subsequent experience is essential for providers working in the human services field, regardless of whether they are asked to deliver specific services intended to address the effects of abuse.

This volume identifies the essential elements necessary for a system to begin to integrate an understanding about trauma into its core service programs. The fundamental elements of a trauma-informed system are identified and the necessary supports for bringing about system change are highlighted. The basic philosophy of trauma-informed practice is then examined across several specific service components: assessment and screening, inpatient treatment, residential services, addictions programming, and case management. In each case the modifications necessary to transform a current system into a trauma-informed system are made explicit. Approaches that then become contraindicated in a trauma-informed program are also identified.

The volume concludes with two chapters that address the changing roles of consumers and providers in a trauma-informed system. Consumers assume a role of greater authority as their voices come to be heard in all aspects of the service delivery process, from designing systems to evaluating the efficacy of those systems. Clinicians also must come to respect and appreciate the impact that trauma has on their own lives as they seek to serve men and women who have been the repeated victims of violence and abuse.

Maxine Harris
Roger D. Fallot
Editors

Work for this issue was supported in part by Grant No. 1 UD1 TI11400-01 to Community Connections from the Substance Abuse and Mental Health Services Administration.

MAXINE HARRIS is codirector of Community Connections in Washington, D.C., and executive director of its National Capital Center for Trauma Recovery and Empowerment.

ROGER D. FALLOT is codirector of Community Connections.

1

With the recognition that large numbers of men and women receiving services in the mental health and addictions systems are the survivors of sexual and physical abuse, practitioners need to become informed about the dynamics and the aftermath of trauma.

Envisioning a Trauma-Informed Service System: A Vital Paradigm Shift

Maxine Harris, Roger D. Fallot

When a consumer seeks services in the mental health or substance abuse treatment systems, it is rarely because he or she wants treatment for current or past sexual or physical abuse trauma. The presenting problems are more immediate and more obviously tied to the stated mission of the service agency. Yet 56 to 63 percent of women seeking inpatient psychiatric services (Bryer, Nelson, Miller, and Krol, 1987) and 40 percent of women in outpatient mental health treatment (Surrey, Suett, Michaels, and Levine, 1990) report some history of abuse in childhood. Victimization rates for a lifetime exposure to trauma among women substance abusers range from 55 to 99 percent (Najavits and others, 1998). And the picture does not look much different for men. Stein and others (1988) report that men with histories of childhood sexual abuse are significantly more likely than their nonabused counterparts to develop a substance abuse disorder; in addition, almost half of them experience a clinical depression at some point in their lives.

Systems *serve* survivors of childhood trauma without *treating* them for the consequences of that trauma; more significant, systems serve individuals without even being aware of the trauma that occurred. This lack of awareness can result in failures to make appropriate referrals for trauma services. It can also result in inadvertent retraumatization when a service system's usual operating procedures trigger a reemergence or an exacerbation of trauma symptoms, as the following examples show:

• A man seeks help because he is anxious and has begun having panic attacks. He is given medication and may be referred to a counselor for therapy sessions, but no one asks him if he was physically abused as a child. The clinic to which he is referred is a large, crowded facility in the center of town. The man must take two buses during rush hour to get there. He goes once but feels too vulnerable and frightened of the clinic environment to continue. After two months, the clinic closes his case.

• A woman and her children seek help because she is feeling overwhelmed and depressed. She has just lost her housing, has been drinking heavily, and cannot concentrate well enough to fill out a job application. She is referred to a family shelter, is given an appointment to meet with a psychiatrist, and talks with an addictions counselor; no one asks her about current domestic violence, much less about any history of childhood sexual abuse. She begins attending an addictions treatment program, but the confrontational style leaves her feeling ashamed and frightened. She loses track of time and misses her appointments. The counselors call her, but she feels too bad about herself to return. After a little more than a month, her case is closed at the addictions program. She is deemed to be insufficiently motivated for treatment.

• A woman is receiving case management services and medication for her schizophrenic illness. She collaborates in her treatment and attends all scheduled meetings. After the Christmas holidays with her family, she begins missing appointments. Her case manager suspects that she is no longer taking her medications. When several attempts to make contact fail, the case manager requests that an emergency psychiatric team go to her home and evaluate her for possible hospitalization. During the evaluation, she becomes verbally abusive; she is restrained, handcuffed, and taken to a state psychiatric hospital. At the hospital, she appears frightened, does not speak, and spends hours staring into space. She remains hospitalized for several weeks. No one who is part of her inpatient or outpatient treatment team knows that she is a survivor of sexual or physical abuse.

In each of these three instances, treatment might have proceeded very differently if the treatment teams had been informed about trauma. By "informed about trauma" we mean two very specific yet different things. First, to be trauma informed means to know the history of past and current abuse in the life of the consumer with whom one is working. Such information allows for more holistic and integrated treatment planning. But second, and more important for this volume, to be trauma informed means to understand the role that violence and victimization play in the lives of most consumers of mental health and substance abuse services and to use that understanding to design service systems that accommodate the vulnerabilities of trauma survivors and allow services to be delivered in a way that will facilitate consumer participation in treatment.

A trauma-specific service is designed to treat the actual sequelae of sexual or physical abuse. Grounding techniques help trauma survivors manage dissociative symptoms, desensitization therapies help to render painful images more tolerable, and certain behavioral therapies teach skills for the modulation of powerful emotions. For a consumer to participate in trauma-specific services, he or she must be aware of a trauma history and recognize current symptoms as sequelae of that trauma. An alert provider may facilitate that awareness and be instrumental in making appropriate referrals.

Trauma-informed services are not designed to treat symptoms or syndromes related to sexual or physical abuse. Rather, regardless of their primary mission—to deliver mental health or addictions services or provide housing supports or employment counseling, for example—their commitment is to provide services in a manner that is welcoming and appropriate to the special needs of trauma survivors.

Perhaps an analogy will make the distinction between a trauma-specific service and a trauma-informed system clearer. The Americans With Disabilities Act (1990) mandated that a wide range of civic and cultural organizations construct their environments so that events are accessible to persons with a range of special needs. As a result, concerts and museums now provide wheelchair access, most theaters have at least one performance that is signed for the hearing impaired, and convenient parking at restaurants is set aside for patrons who cannot walk long distances. These organizations are not delivering specific services for persons with disabilities. Instead, by becoming "disability informed," they are making their services truly available to all people.

Requirements for Creating a Trauma-Informed System of Care

Certain conditions need to be in place for a trauma-informed system to be established. Those conditions reflect the structure and the culture of the organization, and they predate any actual changes in clinical services.

Administrative Commitment to Change. Those who control the allocation of resources within an organization must make a commitment to integrating knowledge about violence and abuse into the service delivery practices of the organization. In the past several years, national initiatives have made it easier for local administrators to do just that. In 1998, the federal government, through a collaborative initiative of the Center for Mental Health Services, the Center for Substance Abuse Treatment, and the Center for Substance Abuse Prevention, funded fourteen sites in the United States to develop integrated services for women who were the victims of violence and were also diagnosed with both a psychiatric illness and a substance abuse problem and for their children. By funding such an initiative, the federal partners were doing more than declaring their interest in violence and victimization in the lives of dually diagnosed women; they were suggesting that violence, addiction, and mental health problems form a complex and interrelated network of connections within the lives of women and within the experience of any given woman. By launching this venture, the federal government made it easier for administrators in public and private agencies around the country to make integrating a trauma perspective an agency priority.

In December 1999, the National Association of State Mental Health Program Directors unanimously passed a resolution recognizing the pervasive impact of violence and trauma. The state directors asserted that recovery from trauma is a fundamental value of mental health providers. Among other things, they were calling for the delivery of trauma-specific services within mental health agencies. Although they did not mention trauma-informed services, they stressed the need for an open discussion and exchange within the public mental health system on the issue of trauma. Such a unanimously passed resolution serves to empower local program directors and providers to emphasize and respect the role that trauma has played and continues to play in the lives of women and men who seek services.

Administrators can declare their intent to make an understanding of the impact of violence and victimization an integral part of the mission of their agencies. This does not necessarily mean that an organization will begin delivering direct trauma services. It simply means that a trauma perspective will be integrated into how staff members understand people and their problems. An administrative commitment to becoming trauma informed begins when the people who allocate resources, set priorities, and sponsor or design programs assert trauma and its aftermath are an important part of what ails people. This statement resonates much more loudly when it is backed up by training, changed policies, new hiring, and enhanced services. But those changes must be preceded by an administrative commitment to change.

Universal Screening. Regardless of their primary mission, all human service agencies can begin by screening individuals seeking services to determine whether they have a trauma history. The screening, administered as quickly as is feasible after an individual enters the service program, can be relatively brief and nonthreatening. An instrument developed at Community Connections in Washington, D.C., consists of only eight items (Fallot, 1999). New enrollees of mental health, addictions, residential services, and homeless outreach programs are asked about witnessed violence, physical abuse, sexual assault, or unwanted sexual touch and threatened violence. An intake worker, a case manager, or a peer advocate can administer the simple screening in a few minutes.

A universal screening furthers the cause of making a system trauma informed in several ways. First, it gets all participants thinking about trauma. Staff members must be conscious of trauma issues because they have to ask the questions, and consumers begin to think about the role that trauma has played in their personal stories. Consumers may also come to see the treatment agency in a more favorable light because staff members care enough to ask about violence and the role that it has played in their lives. Asking about trauma may also lead to more thoughtful referrals for services to trauma-specific treatments.

The very act of asking begins the process of institutionalizing trauma awareness within an agency. The agency—staff, consumers, and administrators—
sees itself as a place where histories of violence and victimization matter. Even
before the agency knows what to do with the information it gathers, it has
become a place where questions that once were taboo are now asked with reg-
ularity and openness and where the stigma surrounding sexual and physical
abuse is beginning to erode.

Training and Education. Regardless of the professional training they
have received, all staff members in a human services agency can benefit
from introductory information about trauma.

When an organization has a commitment to provide trauma services,
the program directors often begin by developing a cadre of trained clinicians who can deliver those services. Specialized training is made available
to those clinicians through seminars, continuing-education efforts, and
ongoing supervision. Although these efforts make trauma-specific services
available, they do not make the entire system trauma informed. Instead,
information about trauma is seen as the special purview of an elite group
of clinicians.

The agency that is determined to inform all of its staff about trauma
dynamics would do well to postpone the intensive training for a few in favor
of a more general introduction for the many. A trauma survivor who seeks
services may interact with a dozen individuals before actually sitting down
with a clinician trained to provide trauma services. A woman will have to
make an appointment and speak with a receptionist. A man will have to enter
the agency and walk past a security guard or a maintenance worker. A family may stop for a snack at the hospital cafeteria. Once they are in the agency,
they may encounter office workers, intake personnel, trainees, and anonymous clinicians. Any one of these individuals has the opportunity to make a
consumer's visit to the service agency inviting or terrifying.

With just a brief introduction to trauma dynamics, all of the personnel
at a service agency can become more sensitive and less likely to frighten or
retraumatize a consumer seeking services. That is not to say that the person
working the elevator should be providing therapy. It is to say, however, that
if a man on the elevator begins to dissociate and forgets what floor he is
looking for, the operator should not treat him with scorn or harshness but
should gently guide him to the appropriate office.

Several curricula exist to introduce human service workers to trauma-
related issues. The "What Is Trauma?" presentation developed at Community Connections (1999a) is a half-day introduction to the symptoms,
feelings, and responses associated with trauma. The more in-depth *Risking
Connection* (Saakvitne, Gamble, Pearlman, and Tabor Lev, 2000) has been
used in several state-wide trainings and outlines the RICH guidelines for
working with the survivors of abuse. RICH stands for the four principles that
are essential in any interaction with a trauma survivor: respect, information,
connection, and hope. The curriculum gives learners a basic understanding

of trauma and its impact and suggests ways in which the RICH guidelines can be part of even the briefest interactions.

Systems can use one of the existing curricula or can devise one more specific to the mission of their agency. A welfare-to-work program, for example, might be most interested in how trauma dynamics look in the workplace. Ultimately the goal might be to assist employment counselors in becoming sensitive to how trauma survivors present themselves to prospective employers as a result of having trauma histories.

For many agency staff, the most powerful training comes from men and women who have experienced and survived trauma. The forty-minute *Women Speak Out* video (Community Connections, 1999b) gives women the opportunity to share how trauma has affected their lives, what symptoms and vulnerabilities they have had to endure, and an opportunity to describe what has been helpful in promoting recovery. When agency staff watch such a video or witness a panel discussion led by trauma survivors and have a chance to ask questions and discuss what they have seen and heard, they move toward becoming trauma sensitive and trauma informed without needing professional-level or in-depth training.

When administrative staff require that all personnel receive a minimum level of training about trauma, the word goes out that making the agency a safe place for trauma survivors is not solely the responsibility of a few clinicians but of everyone who works for the agency and comes in contact with consumers.

Hiring Practices. One obvious way to make a system more trauma informed is to hire workers and clinicians who already have a basic understanding of trauma dynamics. For most agencies, other than those just opening their doors for the first time, such a practice is unfeasible. It is possible, however, to hire one or two trauma champions.

A champion understands the impact of violence and victimization on the lives of people seeking mental health or addictions services and is a front-line worker who thinks "trauma first." When trying to understand a person's behavior, the champion will ask, "Is this related to abuse and violence?" A champion will also think about whether his or her own behavior is hurtful or insensitive to the needs of a trauma survivor. The champion is there to do an identified job—be a case manager or a counselor or a residential specialist—but in addition to his or her job, a champion is there to shine the spotlight on trauma issues.

At Community Connections, a private, not for profit mental health and substance abuse treatment agency in Washington, D.C., a small group of clinicians—one or two on each of several clinical teams—managed to help change the culture of an entire agency. These clinicians, supported by agency directors, reminded all staff of the importance of trauma. In treatment meetings, during collaborations with other agencies, and while attending agency-wide trainings, they could be counted on to ask questions about trauma and suggest ways to support trauma survivors in their recovery efforts. At times they seemed overly zealous, but over time their clear message influenced the practices of others. It became natural for staff other than the champions to include considerations about trauma in their everyday practice.

Review of Policies and Procedures. As a treatment system increases its awareness about and sensitivity to issues of trauma and abuse, it makes sense for administrators, clinicians, and consumers to undertake a careful review of policies and procedures to determine whether any are hurtful or even harmful to trauma survivors—for example, the use of seclusion, physical restraints, strip searches, and involuntary hospitalizations (Carmen and others, 1996). Such policies can be replaced with less intrusive alternatives such as voluntary time-outs, one-on-one support during times of crisis, and advance directives that respect a consumer's preference for how to handle crises.

For many consumers, intrusive practices are both damaging in the moment and painful reminders of past abuses. Psychologist and parent Ann Jennings (1997) describes the flashbacks and numerous setbacks that her daughter Anna experienced as she was retraumatized by standard mental health inpatient practices. Anna Jennings, who had been sexually abused as a child, relived her abuse at the hands of treatment providers who restrained her, stripped her, and secluded her much as her original abuser had.

Even a cursory review of practices and policies might reveal the obvious interventions that are damaging. Review committees also need to be vigilant to identify practices that may replicate trauma dynamics in more subtle ways. For this, the system will need at least one staff member who understands abuse and the systems that, at times unwittingly, support it.

In particular, providers need to be aware of the dynamics that characterize abusive relationships in general and make sure that those same dynamics are not being unwittingly replicated in helping relationships. The following themes characterize abusive relationships:

- Betrayal occurs at the hands of a trusted caregiver or supporter.
- Hierarchical boundaries are violated and then reimposed at the whim of the abuser.
- Secret knowledge, secret information, and secret relationships are maintained and even encouraged.
- The voice of the victim is unheard, denied, or invalidated.
- The victim feels powerless to alter or leave the relationship.
- Reality is reconstructed to represent the values and beliefs of the abuser. Events are reinterpreted and renamed to protect the guilty.

A policy review committee needs to look at current practices and evaluate whether there are traumatic reenactments masquerading as benign practice. For example, outpatient commitments, which make it almost impossible for consumers to leave treatment relationships, may feel to the consumer like the same trap that characterized abusive relationships in childhood when the individual felt powerless to leave or alter the situation.

For systems in which a systematic review of policies is not feasible, two administrative directives might suffice:

Adopt a universal assumption of inclusion; that is, assume that all consumers receiving services are trauma survivors. Clinicians who work in a public sector mental health or addictions program will be only slightly off in terms of an actual head count. Such an assumption might result in the universal elimination of certain aggressive practices that most consumers, trauma survivors or not, find frightening and demeaning. It might also mean that all consumers are treated with more honesty and respect.

Adopt the physicians' credo, *Primum non nocere:* "Above all else, do no harm." Clinicians and other direct service staff should be encouraged to ask themselves whether what they are about to do with, for, or to a consumer might cause harm or, at the very least, more harm than good. Such self-regulation might lead clinicians to question their behavior and thus avoid damaging interactions.

Principles and Philosophy of a Trauma-Informed System

Certainly an administrative commitment to change, the adoption of universal screening practices, training and education for staff, sensitive hiring practices, and a review of policies and procedures assist a system in becoming trauma informed. But true change occurs when the people who make up the system share a philosophy about trauma, services and the service relationship, and consumers that reflects a sensitivity to trauma and its importance in the lives of men and women who seek services.

Understanding Trauma. How clinicians choose to understand trauma will determine to a large measure how they envision the overall treatment of trauma survivors.

The Traditional Approach. Trauma is usually understood as a single event, albeit one with profound impact. The single event that we label as trauma involves actual or threatened death, serious injury, serious harm, or a threat to one's personal integrity. The response to such an event, often diagnosed as a posttraumatic stress disorder, includes intense fear, helplessness, and a sense of unreality or horror (American Psychiatric Association, 1994).

When practitioners talk about the impact of trauma, they generally expect that the impact will be felt in predictable areas of functioning. For example, following a car accident, we might expect that fear and anxiety will be associated with riding in or driving a car. We also expect that responses will follow expected courses. Periods of shock, denial, anger, grief, acceptance, and coping are the loosely organized stages by which individuals come to terms with traumatic events. If the processing of such events exceeds specified time periods, then the conclusion might be that an individual is experiencing a posttraumatic syndrome requiring treatment. And such trauma-specific problems would most likely be treated in mental health clinics, where specially trained practitioners would provide services.

The Trauma-Informed Approach. The understanding of trauma that we are proposing for a trauma-informed system is really quite different. When an individual is bombarded with repeated traumas that constitute threats to his or her personal integrity and worldview, then that individual comes to question even the most fundamental assumptions about the world. In the wake of trauma, that person must construct a new theory of how the world works and how people behave.

Humans seek to make sense out of their experiences, no matter how horrific or bizarre that experience might be. We want things to have meaning, and when events occur that challenge our view of the world, then we must struggle to find a new way to organize and understand our experience.

Consider the case of a young boy who lives with his mother and father. His father dies suddenly one day while driving home from work. The boy and his mother must move to a new apartment because there is now less money for rent. The boy's mother finds a job working evenings and leaves him at home with an aunt, who drinks heavily. One night the aunt's boyfriend gets drunk and begins to beat the boy. When the child tries to defend himself, the man rapes him to "teach him a lesson." The rapes and beatings continue for several months until the mother finds out, and the boy and his mother make other arrangements for his care.

This child initially believed in the safety and security of his world. He viewed adults as caring and protective and events as manageable and predictable. Then tragedy strikes, and the old explanations no longer make sense. The world is dangerous, unsafe, and confusing. The boy must find a new way to explain what has happened. He decides that he is bad and that God is punishing him for misdeeds. He promises himself that he will try to be perfect in every way so that the curse that has befallen him will be lifted and his previous good life will be restored.

As an adult looking at the explanations of a child, we might be tempted to think that he is using magical thinking and that he is assuming almost delusional responsibility for events that are quite obviously out of his control. But the child is not an adult; he is a child, and he is doing his best to make sense of his world.

Many years later, when this same boy, now a young man, seeks services for his overwhelming anxiety and episodic drinking, his view of the world may still reflect some of the explanations he constructed for himself many years earlier. He is a trauma survivor, but he does not seek services for that reason or for anything obviously connected to his abuse history. The early trauma and his attempt to understand it began a complex pattern of actions and reactions that have a continuing impact over the course of his life.

In a trauma-informed system, trauma is viewed not as a single discrete event but rather as a defining and organizing experience that forms the core of an individual's identity. The explanations about abuse, the far-reaching impact, and the attempts to cope with the aftermath come to define who the trauma survivor is. Some trauma survivors report that they feel as if they have lived two lives—one before the trauma occurred and one after—and those two lives seem very different from one another.

Because trauma serves to organize experience, it is misguided for clinicians and consumers to look for its impact in only the obvious places. It makes sense to assume that a girl who was repeatedly raped by a babysitter would have sexual and relationship difficulties. The difficulties of a girl with such a history may be farther reaching and less obviously connected to the abuse, however. If she learned to cope with the abuse by drifting away and dissociating while it was happening, then she may have begun a pattern of losing connection to her experience that, while it served her well during the abuse, may become problematic as she tries to learn algebra or drive to a friend"s house after school. She may now come to a clinic because she has been diagnosed with learning problems, not because she is a trauma survivor. And she may well be treated for those problems without anyone beginning to question how her problems with concentration began.

In a trauma-informed system, practitioners assume that when trauma has occurred, it changes the rules of the game. An individual constructs a sense of self, a sense of others, and a belief about the world after trauma and abuse have occurred that incorporates and is in many cases based on the horrific event or events. That meaning system then informs other life choices and guides the development of particular coping strategies. The impact of trauma is thus felt throughout an individual's life in areas of functioning that may seem quite far removed from the abuse, as well as in areas that are more obviously connected to the trauma.

Understanding the Consumer Survivor. Within human service systems, the recipient of services has been referred to as a patient, a client, a member, and a consumer. These terms reflect the changing view of the person who seeks services, a view that influences all aspects of the service relationship.

Traditional Approach. In most human service settings, the consumer and her problem are synonymous. If someone seeks help for an anxiety disorder, then her identity at the clinic is as a person with symptoms of anxiety. An appreciation of the whole person is often blocked by the importance of the particular, isolated problem.

A woman who had experienced repeated sexual abuse in childhood at the hands of her grandfather sought treatment for anxiety. She had recently been diagnosed with breast cancer, and the medical diagnosis had caused her to become anxious about her health; as important, it had also caused her to revisit the abuse that had included her grandfather's fondling her breasts. When she presented at a mental health clinic, she revealed that she had been drinking to help her get to sleep at night. Within two weeks of seeking help, she was being seen by three separate providers: her surgeon, who saw her as a breast cancer patient; a psychiatrist, who was seeing her to prescribe medication for her anxiety; and a substance abuse counselor, who saw her as a borderline alcoholic. Each provider saw her as the embodiment of certain medical and psychological problems, but none of them saw her as a whole person whose symptoms were interconnected and embedded in her trauma history.

In addition, they approached her problems as if they had a life of their own, independent of context. The self-soothing with alcohol, for example, was seen as substance use on the slippery slope to abuse. No one considered the fact that the use was connected to anxiety over the medical diagnosis and to flashbacks of the sexual abuse. In the traditional approach, symptoms are more likely to be seen as rooted in either biology or character pathology than as responses to particular contexts and circumstances.

There is also a blurring of the distinction between a problem and a symptom in the traditional approach. Many human service providers are trained to treat symptoms rather than to solve problems. If, for example, a man comes to a clinic complaining of sleeplessness, his symptom of sleeplessness may also be considered his problem. The practitioners decide to treat the symptom, which they believe will solve the problem. A careful assessment may reveal, however, that the sleeplessness is in response to the violent behavior of his domestic partner. His symptom is indeed sleeplessness, but his problem is that he is in a violent relationship that he does not know how to get out of. Treating the symptom will leave the problem untouched.

With the emphasis on individually based symptoms in the traditional approach, it is not surprising that the allocation of responsibility to the consumer is often either too great or too little. At times, the consumer is seen as a passive player who must learn to cope with symptoms that are beyond his control. At other times, the consumer is given all the responsibility for solving problems that are embedded in a complex social context. In both cases, the individual is left feeling confused over just how much responsibility she should shoulder.

Trauma-Informed Approach. In a trauma-informed approach, the emphasis is on understanding the whole individual and appreciating the context in which that person is living her life. Rather than asking, "How do I understand this problem or this symptom?" the practitioner now asks, "How do I understand this person?" This approach shifts the focus to the individual and away from some particular and limited aspect of her functioning, and it gives the message that her life is understandable and that behaviors make sense when they are understood as part of a whole picture.

Often trauma survivors think of themselves as a "mess." Events do not seem to make sense, and these survivors see themselves as a chaotic and unpredictable collection of symptoms and responses. As much as needing the solution to a particular problem, trauma survivors need to believe that their behavior is intelligible and capable of being brought under their control. A holistic and trauma-focused understanding gives consumer-survivors a structure for organizing and understanding their experience.

Imagine, for example, trying to read a book that has no plot. There are no organizing themes, no recurrent patterns. Every page has a new and unpredictable set of events that seem unconnected to the events on the previous page, and there is no way of guessing, much less predicting, what will happen next. At first the book might seem entertaining and even exciting, but eventually it just seems like too much effort to read. Now imagine that that book is your life. Nothing makes sense, and you cannot plan or take control of even the simplest activities.

Faced with such a predicament, trauma survivors feel confused, defeated, and depressed. Some become anxious and paranoid because nothing seems to make sense. When presented with a holistic look at their life and struggles, most trauma survivors feel some combination of relief, gratitude, and heightened efficacy. Confusion is replaced by comprehension, and they feel that they can begin to solve individual problems with the belief that their solutions will make sense.

Two related tenets of a trauma philosophy make this transformation possible and plausible. First, trauma-related symptoms arise as attempts to cope with intolerable circumstances, and second, those symptoms emerge in a context of abuse. Consider a young boy whose father beats him for no apparent reason. The father comes home from work, encounters his son playing video games, and flies into a rage. He beats his son hard enough to raise welts on the boy's skin. The boy tries to understand what he did wrong. Maybe he should not have been playing games and instead should have been helping his mother fix dinner. So the next night he is in the kitchen washing vegetables when his father comes home. His father looks at him, flies into a rage, and once again beats him. The boy is frightened and confused. He becomes anxious, hypervigilant, and somewhat suspicious of his father's every move. As he gets older, he discovers that smoking a little marijuana helps him to relax and be less anxious. His behavior, the anxiety, the suspicion, and the substance use all make sense as attempts to cope with his father's irrational behavior.

Now consider his father's behavior. The father grew up with a highly critical grandfather who was disabled and stayed home all day. As soon as his grandson came home from school, the grandfather began a barrage of criticisms. The old man could not leave his chair, but he could unleash a verbal assault that was as vicious as any physical punishment. The boy tried staying late with friends, but his grandfather was waiting for him with a new attack. He asked his mother to intervene, but she passively responded, "You know your grandfather." Finally he started to attack first. His aggressive behavior managed to stifle his grandfather, but it produced conflict with friends and, eventually, his coworkers, and of course it was damaging to his son. If we go back even further, we uncover generations of abuse passed from father to son. And in each generation, we discover attempts to cope—desperate, sometimes irrational, sometimes even abusive—that all originated as attempts to survive and manage the abusive actions of others.

In these stories, we see behaviors as context and relationship dependent. We also see that symptoms begin as attempts to cope. This way of looking at behaviors allows trauma survivors to reclaim the positive coping aspects of their symptoms.

For many girls who were sexually abused, some form of dissociation becomes a way of surviving the abuse. While a girl is being raped, she takes herself, emotionally and psychologically, to another place. If she could, she would remove herself physically, but that is not a possibility, so she closes her eyes and escapes. To be fully present while one is being raped by a trusted schoolteacher is intolerable, so the girl vanishes. And she learns to remove herself easily from all types of unpleasant situations. Unfortunately, she has unleashed a powerful genie. The dissociation happens when she wants to be present—when she is studying for an exam, babysitting for a neighbor, driving home from school. The girl comes to blame herself for being stupid, absentminded, and careless. She does not recognize that that behavior, a creative and clever way to cope with abuse, saved her life a long time ago.

As women come to see the power in their defenses and coping strategies, they also come to believe that they have the strength and the wisdom to make changes in their lives.

Finally, within a trauma-informed system, the consumer-survivor reevaluates her responsibility for the changes and decisions she must make. She is not the passive victim who was abused back then and has no power now; nor is she the fully responsible adult who can take charge now and should have been more forceful back then. The trauma survivor recognizes that the blame for past abuse rests with the perpetrator and the system that allowed the abuse to go on. She also recognizes that the responsibility for change now lies with her and those she chooses to make collaborators in her recovery. The distinction between blame and responsibility allows a trauma survivor to assume balanced and appropriate authority for her future.

Understanding Services. The nature of services delivered by human service agencies can be defined quite narrowly or more broadly, depending on how the agency views its mandate.

Traditional Approach. In a cost-conscious environment, human service providers must define their service commitments within a narrow range. Services, for example, are frequently time limited, and that limitation applies to inpatient psychiatric services as well as to drug treatment programs and outpatient psychotherapies. Because of these limitations, the goal of services must be limited and circumscribed as well. In many cases, the only viable goal is stabilization. Once symptoms have been managed, the treatment ends. In the best of circumstances, the consumer has learned skills or received directives for how to manage the symptoms in the future, but in most cases the consumer leaves only to await a reoccurrence and then a certification for more services.

Not surprisingly, services are often crisis driven in such an environment. The only justification for services is an acute flare-up of symptoms. An alcoholic who is not drinking may be viewed as an inappropriate candidate for drug treatment services even if he is struggling with maintaining his sobriety. Only when there is a relapse will services be authorized and only with the goal of reestablishing sobriety. While the short-term economic justification for such a policy may be understandable, to a trauma survivor such crisis-driven services may recreate troubling dynamics from the past. Many trauma survivors report that as long as they were able to stumble through a day, they were told to "endure the abuse and just get on with things." Only when they felt absolutely desperate, and in many cases suicidal, did anyone pay attention to their distress.

In addition to the concern over costs, the provider in a traditional human services system must be mindful to minimize risk to the system. Some treatment options, which place more autonomy in the hands of the consumer and her network of friends and supporters, may seem overly risky. If, for example, a young woman who is feeling suicidal does not want to be hospitalized and instead wants to stay at home with a good friend who promises to keep her company throughout the night, a provider, worried about potential liability, may opt to go against her wishes and order an involuntary hospitalization. The potential cost to the system of a lawsuit far outweighs the individual's request for an alternative to hospitalization.

Services are thus content specific, time limited, and outcome focused. The individual is identified as suffering from a particular symptom or constellation of symptoms and receives a targeted treatment to address just that problem. Once the symptom is treated and managed, the treatment is over. The goal is stabilization in the most efficient manner with the fewest risks.

Trauma-Informed Approach. The goal of the trauma-informed service system is to return a sense of control and autonomy to the consumer-survivor. A trauma-informed system holds to the underlying belief that if consumers learn to understand and ultimately to control their responses, then they will need less, if any, help from service providers. Like the proverb, 'Give a hungry man a fish, and you feed him today, Teach him to fish, and you feed him forever,' the provider's job becomes helping the consumer to master the skills necessary to cope in healthy and constructive ways. Accordingly, the emphasis is on skill building and acquisition and only secondarily on symptom management. If we assume that some symptoms are misguided attempts to cope, then helping a woman to manage better will obviate the necessity for those symptoms. A woman in a trauma recovery group, for example, stopped using drugs to manage her symptoms when some of those symptoms muted and she concurrently learned other ways to soothe herself.

If services are designed to promote growth and mastery, then it makes sense that service time limits are set in collaboration with the trauma survivor. There are certainly objective indicators that one is functioning better and is more in control of one's behavior and one's environment, but for many women, the sense of having power is a subjective one. A woman has power and mastery in part when she believes that she has those attributes. In fact, telling a woman that she has control when she does not believe that she does reduces her sense of personal efficacy rather than enhancing it. Once again someone else is presuming to know her and what she needs better than she does.

Services in the trauma-informed approach are strengths based. The emphasis is on identifying the capacities a woman or man has used to survive and appreciating how to take those capacities and put them to even better use. If a woman has been guarded and hypervigilant in her approach to other people, then she has had to pay attention to details. She has learned to size up other people and get a quick sense of whom it is safe to trust. She has also demonstrated an ability to protect herself and a willingness to do what it takes to keep herself safe. In these capacities are the beginnings of skills that will help her choose relationships wisely and pay attention in school or on the job. In addition, there may be other skills, such as modulating her anxiety when she becomes frightened, that she will need to learn for the first time.

Ultimately the goal of the services is to prevent problematic behavior in the future—or at the very least to devise a plan for how to deal with crises when they arise. For this reason, initial service contacts may require more time and more intense collaboration than in a traditional approach, but ultimately the consumer-survivor will have the internal and external resources to manage events without the assistance of a service provider. It should be noted that plans to prevent or manage future crises are always driven by the needs and the capacities of the consumer. For some trauma survivors, the very act of devising a crisis prevention plan is sufficient to negate the need for such a plan. Knowing that she has some control over future events helps to decrease a trauma survivor's anxiety and may consequently work to deescalate a difficult situation.

The focus on prevention also has important implications beyond the person seeking services directly. Many trauma survivors come from families and communities where violence and victimization are passed from one generation to the next. When men and women learn to modulate their own responses and to comfort themselves in times of stress, they are better able to parent and protect their children. They may also be better able to recognize the signs of distress in their children once they have learned to identify those markers in their own behavior. Early intervention on behalf of high-risk children may help to end the heartbreaking cycle of transgenerational violence and abuse.

Finally, a trauma-informed system weighs risks to consumers along with risk to providers when making clinical decisions. In the case of a man expressing feelings of despair and talking about ending his life, a service provider may decide that the safest option is to have the man hospitalized.

The consumer, however, may have had a negative experience the last time he was taken to the hospital and may feel that a hospitalization is not only dangerous but also a failure of his own coping skills. Rather than being hospitalized, the man might feel that it is safer to spend the weekend with a good friend who had agreed to be with him and talk through his feelings. Choosing hospitalization minimizes risk to the system; choosing a more nontraditional community alternative minimizes risk to the individual. A collaborative trauma-informed approach would take both of these risks into account and devise a plan that was acceptable to all parties.

Understanding the Service Relationship. Because human services are delivered within the context of a relationship, how providers and consumers understand that relationship can have an important role in defining the services themselves.

Traditional Approach. In many traditional service systems, the consumer is viewed as the passive recipient of services. The specific providers and the care system in general are viewed as possessing superior knowledge and resources. In a mental health system, the providers have an understanding of symptoms, medications, and treatment approaches. They have usually received that knowledge by acquiring formal education and receiving a degree and some official certification such as a license. Because of their knowledge, they are accorded more status in the relationship with the consumer, and their perceptions and opinions receive more weight. Even when there is an attempt to collaborate around treatment decisions and to honor the consumer's choices for his or her life, most consumers perceive traditional mental health relationships as hierarchical.

Providers also hold the key to much-needed resources. They can make referrals to vocational and residential programs. They are often able to determine whether a consumer receives entitlement benefits by how they fill out social security forms. In residential programs, providers may determine whether a consumer has the opportunity to see her family or entertain guests in his room. And on inpatient wards, it is the provider who determines when the individual eats, sleeps, goes to the bathroom, or smokes a cigarette. With providers controlling so many of the resources, it is difficult to imagine real parity between caregiver and consumer. The parity that does exist is often granted by the provider, susceptible to being suspended if the provider feels that the consumer "no longer deserves such a privilege."

It is no wonder that in such a system, consumers often find themselves frightened and cautious. Paradoxically, the "good" consumer does what he is told so that he will be allowed to have a voice in his own care. In such a system, consumers feel that they are ignored and put down, but most learn how to play the game so that they can survive. The very nature of the service relationship makes real collaboration difficult at best.

Regrettably, a relationship with a powerful authority figure who controls all of the resources and whose opinions and wishes take priority over one's own is tragically reminiscent of the abuse dynamic in which the trauma survivor was forced to accept an unequal relationship in order to avoid even worse treatment. The traditional service relationship replicates some of the most damaging dynamics of childhood trauma. The trauma survivor who was unable to stand up for herself as a child may be unable to have autonomous opinions and desires even if the provider assures her that her wishes will be respected.

Even in many addictions programs, where the providers may themselves be people in recovery, the newly admitted consumer will be asked to bend her will to the power of the program. The counselors possess elevated status by virtue of the longevity of their sobriety. They are living proof that their way is the right way. The consumer with too much willfulness will need to turn some of the control for her recovery over to a higher power. While the self-help mantra of many addictions programs has proven useful for many consumers, the model perpetuates the hierarchical service relationship characteristic of most traditional programs. And once again a program that perpetuates the consumer's belief that she does not have the power to help herself or that he does not know his own needs and desires replicates the dynamics of abuse in which a powerful perpetrator proposed to "know what was best."

Because providers in most service systems believe in the integrity and efficacy of their models, they assume that newly admitted consumers will trust the program and feel safe within its borders. Providers are often surprised to learn that rather than entering hospitals, clinics, and rehabilitation programs with a sense of trust and security, many consumers enter with a sense of suspicion and wariness. They may have a prior history of failed or troubled treatment at other service centers. Some feel that prior caregivers betrayed the promise of treatment, and others bring experiences of actual abuse at the hands of service providers. Even if past service experiences were positive, all trauma survivors bring a healthy suspicion of people in authority. Consequently, the provider's assumption of safety and trustworthiness is rarely, if ever, shared by the consumer.

Trauma-Informed Approach. The core of the service relationship in a trauma-informed system is open and genuine collaboration between provider and consumer at all phases of the service delivery. This means that consumers choose where, how, and when they will receive services, and they also have an active voice in deciding on the specific provider. Consumers help to set service priorities, determining which services will be delivered first. For example, a woman who feels that her housing and child care needs require attention before she seeks treatment for her depression will be given the opportunity to specify the order of the services that she receives.

This does not mean that providers will become silent partners in the service relationship. It does mean, however, that a provider will have to explain the rationale behind his or her decisions and that achieving a comfortable compromise with the consumer becomes more important than having one's way. It also means that providers may come to question the reasonableness of doing things in the usual way. Often providers find that things are done the way they have always been done. Routine takes priority over revisiting procedures to determine the best way of delivering services for each individual consumer. Providers may find that in a trauma-informed system, they can be creative about how they deliver services.

When invited to be truly active participants in their treatment, some consumers respond enthusiastically from the beginning. Others are legitimately wary. The invitation to collaborate should always be genuine and must always remain open. Providers should not assume that some initial reticence is an indication that a consumer wants to turn the authority for her treatment over to someone else. It may simply mean that she is unaccustomed to being genuinely included in the plan for her own care.

Trust and safety, rather than being assumed from the beginning, must be earned and demonstrated over time. By beginning a new service relationship with an open question about what the consumer wants and what would help her to feel comfortable and safe, the provider takes the first step toward establishing safety. The provider should also make a clear statement about what he can and cannot do. By eliminating ambiguity and vagueness, the provider once again takes steps to establish trust. Providers realize that the style of interaction is as important in establishing a collaborative relationship as the content of the services delivered.

Providers should also assume that trust is earned over time and not given like a gift on the first meeting. Consequently, in initial meetings, providers should limit the amount of a consumer's disclosure and risk taking. In groups designed to address trauma issues specifically, consumers who disclose too much in the first session often do not return for subsequent sessions. The task of the provider is to make the group a safe place, and she can do that by letting consumers know that personal information is respected. By a simple comment like, "I'd like to hear about that, but why don't you wait until we know each other a little better," the provider demonstrates that she knows she must earn the consumer's trust. The provider also acknowledges that there are stages to a relationship and that closeness and sharing develop over time.

Finally, in a trauma-informed relationship, both parties are acknowledged for bringing valid sources of information and expertise to the relationship. Providers have access to the latest research and have knowledge about innovative clinical programming. They also have expertise based on academic training and eventually on years of practical experience. The provider's knowledge is generic; it applies generally to all consumers with a given history and diagnosis. The consumer's knowledge is, by contrast, very specific. She knows her own responses, her needs, and her history better than anyone else does. She knows, in the words of many consumers, what helps and what hurts. By respecting the consumer's knowledge and her insights about the course of her symptoms and the scope of her attempts to cope and bring order into her life, the provider allows for a truly collaborative service relationship.

Conclusion

The task of making a system trauma informed may at first appear daunting. The shift in philosophy amounts to nothing less than a paradigm shift within service delivery systems. At Community Connections in Washington, D.C., we began the process of becoming trauma informed in the mid-1990s. At first, thinking about trauma and its impact seemed like one more thing to be added to the clinician's assessment of every consumer. Slowly, however, in part because consumers responded so positively to our appreciation of the role that violence and victimization had played and continued to play in their lives, the focus on trauma seemed more integrative and less additive. It was impossible to hear a consumer's story without listening for the story of abuse. Once trauma moved to the center of our understanding, we wanted to develop approaches that would avoid retraumatizing and revictimizing consumers. Without even consciously intending to do so, we evolved the philosophy and principles of a trauma-informed system. It is now unthinkable to return to the traditional way of understanding services and the service relationships in which we participate.

References

American Psychiatric Association. *Diagnostic and Statistical Manual of Mental Disorders.* (4th ed.) Washington, D.C.: American Psychiatric Association, 1994.

Bryer, J., Nelson, B., Miller, J., and Krol, P. "Childhood Physical and Sexual Abuse as Factors in Adult Psychiatric Illness." *American Journal of Psychiatry,* 1987, *144,* 1426–1430.

Carmen, E., and others. *Task Force on the Restraint and Seclusion of Persons Who Have Been Physically or Sexually Abused.* Boston: Massachusetts Department of Mental Health, 1996.

Community Connections. "What Is Trauma?" Training presentation, Community Connections, 1999a.

Community Connections. *Women Speak Out.* Washington, D.C.: Community Connections, 1999b. Videotape.

Fallot, R. "Violence and Trauma Screening Questionnaire for Human Service Agencies." Washington, D.C.: Community Connections, 1999.

Jennings, A. "On Being Invisible in the Mental Health System." In M. Harris and C. Landis (eds.), *Sexual Abuse in the Lives of Women Diagnosed with Serious Mental Illness.* Amsterdam: Harwood Academic Publishers, 1997.

Najavits, L., and others. "The Addiction Severity Index as a Screen for Trauma and Post Traumatic Stress Disorder." *Journal of Studies on Alcoholism,* 1998, *59,* 56–62.

Saakvitne, K., Gamble, S., Pearlman, L. A., and Tabor Lev, B. *Risking Connection: A Training Curriculum for Working with Survivors of Childhood Abuse.* Lutherville, Md.: Sidran Press, 2000.

Stein, J., and others. "Long-Term Psychological Sequelae of Child Sexual Abuse." In G. E. Wyatt and G. J. Powell (eds.), *The Lasting Effects of Child Sexual Abuse.* Thousand Oaks, Calif.: Sage, 1988.

Surrey, J., Suett, C., Michaels, A., and Levine, S. "Reported History of Physical and Sexual Abuse and Severity of Symptomatology in Women Psychiatric Outpatients." *American Journal of Orthopsychiatry,* 1990, *60,* 412–417.

MAXINE HARRIS is codirector of Community Connections in Washington, D.C., and executive director of its National Capital Center for Trauma Recovery and Empowerment.

ROGER D. FALLOT is codirector of Community Connections.

Universal trauma screening and specific trauma assessment methods are necessary to developing collaborative relationships with trauma survivors and offering appropriate services.

A Trauma-Informed Approach to Screening and Assessment

Roger D. Fallot, Maxine Harris

In spite of the prevalence of trauma histories among individuals receiving mental health and substance abuse services, many clinicians acknowledge that significant trauma concerns are frequently overlooked in professional settings. In the assessment process, two broad factors contribute to this relative neglect: underreporting of trauma by survivors and underrecognition of trauma by providers.

Trauma survivors may not report traumatic experiences for a number of reasons. Immediate safety concerns (for example, violent retaliation by abusers or a lack of secure alternative housing) may lead some to withhold salient information. Some trauma survivors fear stigmatizing service system responses that disbelieve or blame the victim or that pathologize attempts to cope with violence. Some feel ashamed about being victimized and about their attendant vulnerability. Some, perhaps especially men, tend to withdraw and isolate themselves rather than talk to others. Childhood experiences of abuse may not be readily remembered, let alone discussed with a clinician who is not yet trusted.

From the provider's perspective, asking about trauma experiences may not be part of usual intake or assessment procedures. Clinicians' lack of training in trauma or their uncertainty about how to respond to abuse-related issues may contribute to the relative absence of such inquiry. Many providers acknowledge their concern that raising questions of trauma with consumers will be "too upsetting" for trauma survivors and that they feel ill equipped as clinicians to respond helpfully. The paucity of accessible and effective trauma services in many areas makes this concern more immediate. Providers are understandably reluctant to identify pressing clinical needs for which there are no corresponding interventions available. On this, trauma survivors are often in agreement with clinicians: it may be better *not* to ask about trauma if no helpful responses are forthcoming. Even when clinicians ask about violence, they may use overly general and somewhat vague terms like *trauma* or *abuse* that are not meaningful to many trauma survivors. Survivors, for example, may have labeled violent physical abuse in childhood as "discipline" and respond in the negative to inquiries about "childhood abuse." A final institutional factor may lead initial assessments away from a focus on trauma. If certain Axis I disorders are necessary for reimbursement, certification for consumer entitlements, or research, initial assessments may center primarily on identifying only those diagnoses and neglect others, such as posttraumatic stress disorder (PTSD), that will not meet necessary criteria.

Trauma Screening

Trauma screening refers to a brief, focused inquiry to determine whether an individual has experienced specific traumatic events. Because of both underreporting and underrecognition, trauma-informed service systems have increasingly adopted universal screening, asking all consumers about trauma, as part of the initial intake or assessment process. The primary purpose is to determine appropriate follow-up and referral, including urgent responses to imminent danger. In addition to identifying people whose histories call for trauma-specific services, such screening communicates to all consumers that the program believes that abuse and violence are significant events and that staff are willing to discuss trauma with survivors. Even if a trauma survivor decides not to talk about such experiences with staff at this early stage, staff have increased the possibility of later disclosure by communicating their recognition of and openness to hearing about painful events.

Effective trauma screening does not need to be complicated; it does need to be clear. While the range of events included in such screens may be quite broad, covering natural disasters, serious accidents, and deaths of loved ones, here we focus primarily on physical and sexual abuse and violence because they are often a clear priority in initial service planning. Usually screening is limited to several questions. In terms of physical abuse, staff may ask whether an individual has ever been beaten, kicked, punched, or choked. Addressing sexual abuse, they may ask about consumers' experiences of being touched sexually against their will or whether anyone has ever forced them to have sex when they did not want to. If the consumer reports such events, the screening interviewer may ask about recency (In the past six months?) and current danger (Are you afraid now that someone may hurt you?). By using unambiguous and straightforward language, trauma screening avoids confusion about the events the clinician has in mind, and it encourages equally straightforward responses.

This is not to say that asking questions about potentially emotion-laden events should be done without adequate clinical preparation. When a committee of human service professionals and consumer-survivors developed an eight-question screening instrument for distribution in Washington, D.C., they placed considerable emphasis on the need for sensitivity to individual needs and to contextual issues in the screening process. For instance, the committee recommended interviewer training to maximize clinician competence in dealing with the full range of survivor responses to trauma questions. While trauma screening should be done as early as possible in the intake process, there may be good reasons in some settings not to ask about violent victimization in the initial meeting; timing should fit with the needs of the consumer in the larger assessment process. It is important, especially in the event of a negative screen, to repeat the brief set of questions periodically. As trauma survivors develop a sense of safety and trust with providers, they may become more willing to disclose any history of trauma. The committee also recommended several ways to maximize consumer choice and control in the screening process: explaining directly the reasons for the screen and offering explicit options of not answering questions, delaying the interview, self-administering the questionnaire, or having something to drink (coffee or juice) during the screening. The key point of such recommendations is not so much in the specific alternatives offered as in the priority these choices place on consumer preferences regarding self-protection and self-soothing needs. Concluding the brief interview with a discussion of its implications for service planning (and any urgent intervention) begins to connect trauma concerns with the rest of the consumer's problems and goals.

Trauma-informed service systems adopt universal trauma screening, then, not only because of the prevalence of violence or only because of the often powerful impact of abuse but also because trauma screening communicates institutional awareness of and responsiveness to the role of violence in the lives of consumers. Asking about trauma is an invitation to survivors, who may be understandably reluctant or unable to talk about abuse early in the service relationship, to disclose abuse experiences when they feel the necessary sense of safety and trust.

Trauma Assessment

Trauma assessment, in contrast to trauma screening, is a more in-depth exploration of the nature and severity of traumatic events, the sequelae of those events, and current trauma-related symptoms. In the context of a comprehensive mental health assessment, the trauma information may contribute to a formal diagnostic decision.

Assessment as a Process. Trauma-informed assessment often sets an important tone for the early stages of consumer engagement. It is built on the development, rather than the assumption, of safety and trust. Clinicians need to be aware of the understandable fears many trauma survivors bring to situations that call for self-disclosure. At the same time, some survivors, because of boundary difficulties that impair self-protection and the intensity of their trauma experiences, may be unable to modulate their responses to clinician inquiries. They then may find themselves overwhelmed by the emotional impact of telling too much of their own stories. Helping trauma survivors contain and manage the intense feelings that may accompany trauma stories is a key clinical skill; grounding and centering techniques are important resources in such assessment situations.

Exploration of trauma thus unfolds over time, and the clinician, after making it clear that he or she is open and responsive to abuse disclosure, should follow the trauma survivor's lead in this unfolding process. For individuals whose experiences of powerlessness and lack of choice have been pervasive, having control over the pace and content of trauma discussions is very important. Clinicians can contribute to trauma survivors' sense of control by being clear about the steps and process of assessment ("I would like to ask you some questions about . . . "); the reasons for those questions ("We have found that many people who come here for services have been physically or sexually abused at some time in their lives. Because this can have such important effects on people's lives, we ask everyone about whether they have ever been a victim of violence or abuse"); and the consumer's right not to answer questions ("If you would rather not answer any question, just let me know, and we'll go on to something else"). A respectful collaboration in the assessment of abuse and violence sets the stage for shared decision making in the service relationship.

Trauma and Related Diagnoses. Recent summaries of PTSD assessment have emphasized the wide range of conditions that often accompany posttraumatic disorders (Newman, Kaloupek, and Keane, 1996) and the importance of attention to these additional problems in making decisions about treatment (Shalev, Friedman, Keane, and Foa, 2000). Rates of major depression, anxiety disorders, substance abuse, and personality disorders are especially high among those diagnosed with PTSD.

As trauma moves from a more circumscribed and marginal interpretive position to a more central one in a trauma-informed system, though, many co-occurring difficulties may be more helpfully understood as adaptations to traumatic events. Herman and van der Kolk (1987), for example, have described some of the connections between aspects of borderline personality disorder and trauma. They argue that both splitting and self-mutilation may be seen as attempts to come to terms with the biopsychological disruptions that especially attend prolonged early trauma in relationships with caregivers. Self-injuring behavior, then, may be an attempt at self-regulation when other regulatory mechanisms and skills are undeveloped or inaccessible. Similarly, substance abuse may have originated in attempts to numb the psychic pain associated with trauma. Some hallucinatory experiences may be more accurately characterized as PTSD flashbacks than as signs of schizophrenia.

These observations about apparently trauma-based origins of later problems or "symptoms" carry several implications. First, extensive comorbidity of trauma-related and other disorders makes careful attention to differential diagnosis a necessity. Misdiagnosis and underestimation of trauma symptoms are significant concerns. Clinical reports have documented the many diagnoses given to survivors—diagnoses that fail to take into account the trauma experiences themselves (see, for example, Jennings, 1997). Especially among individuals with extensive psychiatric histories, previous documented diagnoses may become self-perpetuating, dominating and prematurely foreclosing the assessment process. A trauma-informed diagnostic assessment, then, takes seriously the wide range of problems that may flow from experiences of violence.

Second, and especially important in terms of fostering collaborative relationships with trauma survivors, framing many "symptoms" as understandable attempts to cope with or adapt to overwhelming circumstances is both more empathic and potentially empowering for trauma survivors. For a trauma-informed assessment, reaching a diagnosis becomes a decidedly secondary goal. The primary goal is the development with the trauma survivor of a shared understanding of the role that trauma has played in shaping the survivor's life. Such an understanding stays closer to trauma survivors' experiences and recognizes the latent strengths in coping attempts. Rather than seeing their "symptoms" and "disorders" as simply more evidence of their fundamental defects, trauma survivors are invited to understand the strengths as well as the limitations growing out of their responses to traumatic events. Dissociation, for example, may have been a valuable, if not essential, tool for survival in abusive, life-threatening circumstances. Similar dissociation generalized to other settings like school or work, though, may have carried decidedly negative consequences. An assessment that communicates this two-sided nature of many trauma responses addresses more effectively both the adaptive capacities and the weaknesses resulting from the trauma survivor's efforts to deal with often horrific events.

PTSD and Complex PTSD. Numerous structured interviews and questionnaires have been developed to assess PTSD (see Keane, Weathers, and Foa, 2000, for an overview). A focus on PTSD and its diagnostic criteria has several advantages: increasing the reliability and validity of assessment techniques, clarifying prevalence and impact data, and providing standardized methods for evaluating the effectiveness of treatment. But the current conceptualization of PTSD as a diagnostic category may also limit recognition and exploration of more complicated, expansive, and long-term effects of trauma (Brett, 1996). In the past decade, theorists have paid increasing attention to the diversity and complexity of adaptations to trauma over longer periods of time (van der Kolk, 1996). This expanded view carries with it important implications for trauma-informed assessments. First, as we noted in Chapter One, there is greater awareness that trauma may constitute a core, life-shaping experience with complicated and shifting sequelae over the course of one's life. This understanding stands in contrast to a more traditional view of trauma as a discrete event with a definable course and relatively circumscribed time limits. Second, while the impact of trauma has often been seen as limited to predictable life domains directly connected to the traumatic event, there is growing recognition that the effects of trauma may appear in multiple life domains that may not be apparently related to the traumatic event.

As part of these enlarged understandings, a trauma-informed assessment recognizes the importance of Complex PTSD (Herman, 1992) or Disorders of Extreme Stress Not Otherwise Specified (van der Kolk, 1996). Fundamental changes in the trauma survivor's affect regulation, consciousness, self-perception, perception of the perpetrator, relations with others, and systems of meaning are characteristic of this larger syndrome (Herman, 1992). Especially in the public service sector, where trauma is pervasive and often related to repeated or longstanding exposure to violence, Complex PTSD captures much more effectively the experience of many trauma survivors than does the more specific PTSD diagnosis.

A trauma-informed approach to diagnosis, then, recognizes the tremendous diversity, range, and duration of trauma sequelae and places these sequelae in the context of the person's life history. Understanding that experiences of physical, sexual, and emotional abuse can shape fundamental patterns of perceiving the world, other people, and oneself, this framework prioritizes exploring the possible role of trauma in the development of not only "symptoms" and high-risk or self-defeating behaviors but of self-protective and survival-ensuring ones. It incorporates these possibilities in a shared assessment process, collaborating with the trauma survivor in discussing and clarifying connections and sequences in the relationships among trauma, coping attempts, and personal strengths and weaknesses.

Assessment of Trauma Histories and Impact. A more complete trauma-informed assessment moves well beyond screening and diagnostic decisions to include a number of factors central to understanding the specific traumatic events the individual has experienced and the impact of those events.

Range of Abusive or Traumatic Experiences. Most definitions of trauma involve two dimensions. First, trauma refers to events that involve actual or threatened death or injury or threats to physical integrity (Criterion A1 in the definition of PTSD; American Psychiatric Association, 1994). In addition, trauma refers to the experiences of helplessness, fear, and horror these events elicit among trauma survivors (Criterion A2). But such definitions do not necessarily yield clarity about whether a particular experience should be considered "traumatic" or "abusive" and often do not reflect the ways in which trauma survivors talk about such events.

In understanding the often complex role of trauma in the lives of survivors, trauma-informed assessment attends to both the reported events and the experiences and meanings connected to those events. Trauma survivors may have learned to normalize or minimize sexual or physical abuse. A male perpetrator, for example, may have convinced a sexually abused girl that unwanted sex was merely part of her "education." Some men may understand being pressured to have sex as a twelve-year-old by an eighteen-year-old female babysitter as simply early sexual initiation rather than a sexual abuse of power. Boys' experiences of helplessness and shame in this situation may be complicated by cultural expectations that "men" are always interested in and available for sex. In a similar way, a culture of violence among men may contribute to boys' acceptance of physical abuse as an accepted part of growing up male; some men express gratitude to their abuser for "toughening them up" or "preparing them for the world." Clinicians need to be aware, therefore, that trauma survivors may not share their views about what constitutes abuse or trauma. A sensitive exploration of both what happened and how it was experienced and understood can create the grounds for more effective services.

Dimensions Related to Severity of Impact. In ongoing discussions with trauma survivors, special attention should be paid to factors that may contribute to more severe long-term sequelae. Some structured interviews and inventories address these dimensions directly. Abuses that began earlier in life, persisted over time, and occurred frequently may have especially negative impact. Assessment should attend to the invasiveness, degree of violence, and potentially life-threatening aspects of abusive events and to the trauma survivor's relationship with the abuser (family member, trusted adult, or stranger), as well as relationship intensity and quality. Very importantly, the responses of other adults to traumatic events and to the trauma survivor's disclosure should be understood in the assessment process. Trauma Survivors consistently report the debilitating effects of being disbelieved or of having their accounts minimized and dismissed as inconsequential. On the other hand, recovery stories often begin with the experience of having an adult advocate who took the abuse seriously, protected the child from further exposure, and sought appropriate help.

Life Domains Affected by Trauma. Assessment should certainly address the core PTSD criteria of reexperiencing, arousal, and avoidance. However, as noted in Chapter One and in the discussion of Complex PTSD, trauma sequelae may be seen in a wide range of life domains and affect a survivor in ways not apparently related to abuse or violence. Trauma-informed assessment looks for these nonobvious connections.

Identification of Current Triggers or Stressors. In addition to historical information, trauma-informed assessment includes an exploration of current circumstances that may trigger trauma responses. While this information is especially valuable in inpatient and residential settings, outpatient programs can work with trauma survivors to develop plans for responding to specific identified stressors. As with other sequelae of abuse, some triggers are readily identified with the original trauma—unexpected touching, threats or loud arguments, violations of privacy or confidentiality, being in confined spaces with strangers, or sexual situations. Others may be less easily connected to the trauma survivor's history. These may become evident only as the clinician comes to know the consumer better and as the trauma survivor comes to recognize and label her or his individual stress responses more accurately.

Identification of Coping Resources and Strengths. Many human service system assessments focus almost exclusively on problems, deficits, and weaknesses. A trauma-informed assessment takes a whole-person approach, expanding its purview to highlight trauma survivors' strengths and resources as well. As certain symptoms are reframed to recognize their origins in attempts to cope with extreme threats and violence, a catalogue of existing coping skills may begin to take shape. Survival itself is often a significant achievement, as are self-protection skills, assertiveness, and self-soothing. Assessment should explore the often nonobvious advantages of specific coping responses and work with the trauma survivor to affirm positive responses and incorporate them into ongoing service plans. Trauma survivors also often bring important personal and interpersonal resources that are not related to their trauma histories. Identifying sources of social support (including safe and trustworthy relationships and places), self-esteem and resilience, self-comforting, and a sense of meaning and purpose helps trauma survivors to recognize and begin to draw on often underused strengths. In terms of current stressors, trauma survivors can also identify strategies that have been helpful to them in dealing with overwhelming emotions. These strategies can become part of the shared service plan (as advance directives) so that professional responses to crises can draw on the trauma survivor's own knowledge of what has previously helped and hurt.

Conclusion

Universal screening helps to identify consumers who may benefit from trauma-specific services and makes it clear that clinical programs take seriously the importance of traumatic events. Trauma-informed assessments are opportunities not only for essential information gathering but for beginning the development of safe, trusting, and collaborative relationships between trauma survivors and clinicians.

References

American Psychiatric Association. *Diagnostic and Statistical Manual of Mental Disorders.* (4th ed.) Washington, D.C.: American Psychiatric Association, 1994.

Brett, E. "The Classification of Posttraumatic Stress Disorder." In B. A. van der Kolk, A. C. McFarlane, and L. Weisaeth (eds.), *Traumatic Stress.* New York: Guilford Press, 1996.

Herman, J. *Trauma and Recovery.* New York: Basic Books, 1992.

Herman, J., and van der Kolk, B. A. "Traumatic Origins of Borderline Personality Disorder." In B. A. van der Kolk (ed.), *Psychological Trauma.* Washington, D.C.: American Psychiatric Press, 1987.

Jennings, A. "On Being Invisible in the Mental Health System." In M. Harris and C. Landis (eds.), *Sexual Abuse in the Lives of Women Diagnosed with Severe Mental Illness.* Amsterdam: Harwood Academic Publishers, 1997.

Keane, T. M., Weathers, F. W., and Foa, E. B. "Diagnosis and Assessment." In E. B. Foa, T. M. Keane, and M. J. Friedman (eds.), *Effective Treatments for PTSD*. New York: Guilford Press, 2000.

Newman, E., Kaloupek, D. G., and Keane, T. M. "Assessment of Posttraumatic Stress Disorder in Clinical and Research Settings." In B. A. van der Kolk, A. C. McFarlane, and L. Weisaeth (eds.), *Traumatic Stress*. New York: Guilford Press, 1996.

Shalev, A. Y., Friedman, M. J., Keane, T. M., and Foa, E. B. "Integration and Summary." In E. B. Foa, T. M. Keane, and M. J. Friedman (eds.), *Effective Treatments for PTSD*. New York: Guilford Press, 2000.

van der Kolk, B. A. "The Complexity of Adaptation to Trauma: Self-Regulation, Stimulus Discrimination, and Characterological Development." In B. A. van der Kolk, A. C. McFarlane, and L. Weisaeth (eds.), *Traumatic Stress*. New York: Guilford Press, 1996.

ROGER D. FALLOT is codirector of Community Connections in Washington, D.C.

MAXINE HARRIS is codirector of Community Connections and executive director of its National Capital Center for Trauma Recovery and Empowerment.

Inpatient hospitalizations can be difficult for the survivors of sexual and physical abuse unless practitioners take care to make the hospital stay trauma informed.

Trauma-Informed Inpatient Services

Maxine Harris, Roger D. Fallot

A trauma-informed psychiatric hospitalization is almost an oxymoron because within a trauma-informed system, hospital treatment should be used infrequently, if at all. A system of care should have a range of alternatives for managing symptomatic behavior and periods of acute distress that are far less restrictive and more consumer controlled than hospitalizations are designed to be.

The following discussion will therefore begin with a consideration of these community-based and consumer-initiated alternatives to inpatient hospitalization, will continue with a discussion of trauma-informed inpatient practices, including a plan for an ideal trauma treatment unit, and will conclude with a discussion of those to-be-avoided practices that can make hospital treatment a retraumatizing experience for trauma survivors.

Alternatives to Hospitalization

Most people who have experienced repeated sexual and physical abuse have periods when they feel out of control and in need of assistance in managing their lives. Trauma survivors can have control over those periods by preparing for them in advance. Mary Ellen Copeland (1997), a writer and consumer-survivor, developed the Wellness Recovery Action Plan intended to help consumers plan for times when they might need extra help in maintaining control over their lives. The plan, to be written when things are going well, begins with a consumer's identifying those things that she needs to do every day to keep feeling healthy—for example, taking a hot shower, taking medication, and talking with a friend or counselor. The list helps trauma survivors acknowledge that they have skills, resources, and capacities to keep themselves feeling well. The plan also helps trauma survivors to feel that what happens to them is under their own control, a feeling very different from the original experience of trauma in which everything seemed, and in many cases was, under the control and the direction of a powerful other person.

The recovery plan continues by having trauma survivors identify events that trigger feeling out of control. For some, the trigger may be an external event like an anniversary date; for others, it may be an internal feeling like guilt or anxiety. For many, there will be more than one trigger, and trauma survivors are encouraged to identify as many as possible. By identifying triggers, trauma survivors learn that behaviors are understandable and learn how to make sense of the triggers as an early warning system that allows them to take action to avoid a decompensation. Copeland follows the identification of triggers with a section in which trauma survivors plan actions that will help to restore equilibrium—for example, exercising, writing in a journal, or talking with a counselor. In all of the directives of the action plan, the emphasis is on empowering trauma survivors to take control of even the most trying of circumstances. Trauma and abuse leave men and women feeling that life "happens to them." Active planning for even the most difficult of circumstances replaces that feeling of helplessness with a sense of active problem solving and realistic control.

Every Wellness Recovery Action Plan concludes with a personal crisis plan in which an individual instructs others on the actions she wants taken if all her prior planning fails and she is unable to take care of herself. This part of the plan includes a list of behaviors that the consumer finds comforting, as well as a list of people who have been helpful in the past. If hospitalization should prove necessary, the plan includes instructions on which hospital to use, which medications are preferred, and which providers are helpful. The plan also includes instructions on who and what should be avoided in a time of crisis, as well as instructions on when a trauma survivor believes that she has regained control and will be able to continue her recovery without further help.

In a trauma-informed system, every trauma survivor should complete a Wellness Recovery Action Plan that includes a crisis plan. When these plans are in place, a consumer and the providers he or she chooses to include will have a range of options for dealing with out-of-control feelings and behaviors, making it rarely, if ever, necessary to require a hospital stay.

Some of the options included in many crisis plans should also be part of the formal structure and care options of any trauma-informed system. Many trauma survivors, for example, prefer being able to spend time with a companion, a friend, or a mental health professional who knows how to help them calm down when they are especially stressed. The care system can have available a cohort of peer companions and crisis specialists who are available for twenty-four-hour one-to-one support. Those companions can be instructed in what strategies are most helpful in allowing the individual to regain control. Some trauma survivors want to be able to talk through their concerns, while others prefer to have quiet company. Some want to be held or touched, while others just want to know that someone else is in the same room. Peer companions and crisis specialists can be available to provide support in an individual's home, so that additional external disruption does not have to accompany whatever inner turmoil the individual is contending with.

In some outpatient settings, hospitalizations can be avoided if therapists are available to help consumers work through an immediate crisis. Linehan (1993) suggests that a hospitalization short-circuits an opportunity for learning and growth. By remaining in a stressful environment, a consumer can come to understand the events that act as triggers and can have the experience of mastering a difficult situation. Linehan even suggests that removing an individual from a difficult situation sets back the cause of growth and empowerment rather than aiding in recovery.

If removal from a home environment is necessitated because an individual cannot care for himself, then the alternative of a community-based crisis house should be considered as an option. In a community-based program, where from two to six individuals receive respite care and supervision, the consumer has a chance to be in a safe environment while regaining control. The crisis house is typically a home in a residential neighborhood, indistinguishable from other residences. It carries none of the stigma of a hospital. The consumer in a crisis program has the opportunity to decide which of her routine activities she wants to resume and when she feels able to resume them. Some will decide to continue working or attending school while in the crisis program. Consumers have an opportunity to process their feelings and behaviors and consider new ways for handling stress while feeling safe and cared for.

Unlike a hospitalization, a stay in a crisis house gives a consumer the sense that he or she can receive some care and support without needing a locked ward. Often trauma survivors see a crisis as a slippery slope. Once things start to go badly, they end in a disaster. A crisis program may give trauma survivors the sense that a small crisis can be managed before it becomes a big crisis. This appreciation of events on a continuum from somewhat difficult to totally unmanageable begins to give trauma survivors a greater sense of realistic control over the events in their lives.

Trauma-Informed Inpatient Services

Even when the consumer and his or her provider network make great efforts to ensure alternatives to inpatient hospitalization, the time may come when the resources, structure, and support of a hospital are necessary for a consumer to get through a particular crisis. The decision to use inpatient hospitalization should always be made with the collaboration and full informed consent of the consumer. Moreover, rather than being seen as a failure on the part of the consumer to take care of herself, a hospitalization should be understood by the consumer, her supporters, and the inpatient treatment staff as an attempt on the part of the consumer to keep herself safe and get the care that she needs. This reframing of the meaning of the hospitalization should not be seen as a linguistic trick. Rather, in a trauma-informed system, providers operate from a strengths-based perspective that allows them to see the coping and problem solving inherent in all behaviors. When the hospitalization is under the control of the consumer and her pre-arranged crisis plan and when she is encouraged to see the choice to be hospitalized as a courageous attempt to manage out-of-control feelings or behaviors, the shame and stigma attached to being hospitalized may at least partially be removed.

Once a consumer enters a hospital, every attempt should be made to respect his or her history of sexual and physical abuse. If the consumer has been at the same hospital previously, prior, accurate records should be used so that a consumer does not have to repeat her trauma story. Consumers feel invisible when they are required to answer the same questions that they have answered during prior admissions. If a consumer is entering a hospital for the first time, designated staff should ask if there is a history of prior or ongoing physical or sexual abuse. Questions should be asked in a straightforward and direct way, and the consumer's preference to skip particular questions should always be honored. The purpose of this trauma screening is not to have someone tell a story of abuse, but rather to get information that might better inform the inpatient stay. In fact, consumers should not be encouraged to go into detail about their histories during the early assessment phase.

The first agenda of an inpatient stay should be to ensure the safety of the consumer. Providers cannot assume that the hospital represents a safe place for a trauma survivor of trauma. A consumer may have had prior experiences with hospitals that cause her to be frightened from the beginning of her admission. Even if a consumer has not had prior bad experiences, the atmosphere of the hospital, which can seem quite intimidating, and the separation from one's own home environment may be sufficient to make the consumer fearful and distrustful.

Ensuring Physical Safety. When considering a consumer's physical safety, providers must be mindful of safety issues both inside and outside the hospital. For example, a woman may be admitted to a hospital following a suicide attempt. The attempt on her own life, however, may have followed a brutal fight with her boyfriend in which he threatened to kill her and her children if she did not give him all of her money to pay a drug debt. While hospitalized, a woman may be terrified of returning home and may be frantic about the safety of her children. A safety plan for when she leaves the hospital is part of helping her to feel safe while she is in the hospital. Such a plan will require not only the involvement of social services, residential services, and possibly child protective services, but also legal counsel and assistance with securing a restraining order to keep the boyfriend away from the consumer and her children (Wile, 1997).

In a trauma-informed system, providers respect the reality of a woman's life circumstances. Her "psychological" issues are not treated in isolation. A provider who wanted to treat the woman's depression with medication and who saw her suicide attempt as a manipulative attempt to punish her boyfriend would be ignoring the role that violence and victimization played in the lives of the consumer and her children. A trauma-informed approach places behaviors in context and helps the woman plan for her safety and the safety of her children.

Providers also need to take steps to ensure a woman's safety while she is hospitalized. This does not solely mean keeping a violent boyfriend from entering the ward, although that is important. It also means making sure that the hospital environment itself is a safe and comforting place. This requirement may leave some staff members perplexed because they have come to take the safety of their work environment for granted. A setting that feels safe to employees may not feel safe to a consumer-survivor, however.

The following practices help to ensure the physical safety of consumers requiring inpatient treatment:

• *Availability of same-gender staff.* In times of distress, both male and female consumers may prefer the option of being treated by same-gender staff. For women who have been abused by a man, a male staff member may trigger frightening memories of past abuses. It may be difficult for the consumer to believe that the staff person truly wants to help and does not want to harm her in some way.

Many male trauma survivors, regardless of the gender of their abuser, report being frightened of women, who can seem all-powerful and intimidating. Moreover, it may seem shameful to a male trauma survivor to acknowledge his vulnerabilities, much less his abuse history, to a female caretaker (Freeman and Fallot, 1997).

The comments about same-gender staff should not constitute an absolute rule. Obviously some female trauma survivors feel more comfortable with a male clinician, and some male survivors prefer talking to a female staff member. What is clear, however, is that in a trauma-informed system, the consumer's preferences about working with a same-sex staff member should be honored, and the option for a same-sex pairing should be made available to all consumers.

• *Separation of male and female consumers.* Ideally men and women should be treated on separate inpatient wards. When that is not possible, some form of physical separation should be established on a single ward. Separate corridors, bathrooms, sleeping quarters, and living room space should be made available. Separate space helps to lessen the chance that consumer-to-consumer abuse will occur on the ward. Regrettably, even on wards with adequate staff supervision, rapes and other acts of violence do occur. Such events, while obviously devastating for the people involved, are also traumatizing for other consumers on the ward at the time (Wile, 1997). Any event of abuse should be followed by appropriate action and an adequate opportunity to process the event by all members of the inpatient community.

• *Availability of safe and comfortable time-out space.* When people are experiencing emotional distress, they may need a place to be alone with their own thoughts and feelings. The space should be small without being claustrophobic; a room eight by ten feet is more than adequate. The room should be furnished with comfortable seating, have adequate lighting, and be comfortably heated or cooled depending on the season. The room should not be overly cluttered with objects or decorations that might be overstimulating, nor should it be austere. A soothing paint color or fabric on the walls can help make the room feel like a safe and gentle place. Consumers should be able to enter the quiet room if they choose without having to gain staff permission. Rooms should be open and, where fire codes permit, should not have a door that locks. When quiet rooms resemble seclusion rooms or cells, they tend to go unused by consumers.

The inclusion of time-out space on an inpatient ward may be met with concern on the part of staff. Staff may worry that the room will allow consumers too much freedom to hide or avoid treatment. In a trauma-informed service, however, the rights of consumers to feel safe and to have some control over their treatment are paramount. Quiet space allows consumers to determine when they need to be alone and when it makes sense to decrease the impact of external and interpersonal stimulation. Learning to read their own internal cues and need states better also may help consumers to avoid the need for future inpatient stays.

• *Respect for personal space and individual boundaries.* A consumer's need and desire for privacy is often at odds with inpatient staff members' needs for information and control of the physical environment. For example, should staff be able to enter a consumer's room without knocking? Under what circumstances should staff be allowed to search a consumer's belongings or her person for contraband? Many of the most stressful experiences that consumers have while on inpatient wards come from these violations of personal space. Yet staff may be legitimately concerned about the consumer's safety, the safety of other residents on the ward, and their own safety as well.

First, it should be a principle of a trauma-informed system to violate personal boundaries as little as possible. Second, if boundaries need to be broken, then staff should explain to the consumer what they are doing and why they are doing it. An explanation, delivered in a calm and respectful way, may help temper the distress that a consumer experiences when she feels intruded on. Staff should remember that trauma violates the most personal of boundaries. Trauma survivors thus may come to long for privacy while expecting intrusions and interruptions. Some trauma survivors may even express confusion over what constitutes a healthy boundary and over their rights to ask for reasonable limits. Orientation to an inpatient unit should also include some discussion of personal space, as well as those circumstances that will cause staff to take control of the physical environment.

Each individual, on being admitted to the inpatient unit, should be given a chance to express preferences for or concerns about interpersonal closeness. Some people like to be touched and approached, while others require a fair amount of distance in order to feel safe. Whenever possible, the consumer's wishes about space should be respected.

• *Respect for personal modesty.* Many trauma survivors feel safe only when they are wrapped in layers of clothing. Having one's body exposed and seen can feel like a retraumatization. Yet inpatient units may require that consumers bathe in communal showers, sleep in gowns that open in the back, and strip for medical exams in rooms that do not have adequate privacy. On a trauma-informed unit, staff need to be aware that sexual and physical abuse violated the consumer's most basic rights to control her body. Policies and procedures concerning bathing, sleeping, and using the bathroom should grant trauma survivors as much control over their own bodies and their bodily functions as is possible.

• *Training for staff in the strategies of safe deescalation.* On any inpatient unit, there are times when people lose control and need assistance in helping to regain composure and restore calm. When staff have no strategies for assisting consumers other than using restraints and physical force or intimidation, they will regrettably resort to those tactics. Visalli, McNasser, Johnstone, and Lazzaro (1997) suggest that staff members be trained to use a five-step approach that only rarely reaches step five (the use of physical restraints). In the first step, staff members are taught to offer consumers a range of tactics for regaining control, such as listening to music, taking a walk, exercising, counting out loud, or talking to a companion. During this step, staff may also offer consumers a blanket to wrap themselves in or a hand to hold. In the second step, the consumer is offered a change of environment, such as a quiet room, another ward, or a chance to take a walk outside. If something in the immediate environment is triggering distress, then the staff person helps the consumer to exit the environment safely until the impact of the trigger dissipates. In step three, the consumer is offered medication to help calm down. Medications are not forced or given involuntarily; the consumer is given the choice to use extra or one-time medication. In the fourth step the consumer is placed in a seclusion room, and in the final step, restraints are used.

The purpose of the step training is to increase the use of strategies in steps one through three and to decrease or even eliminate the use of steps four and five. When consumers know that staff will help them to feel calm in the least violent and intrusive way possible, they are more likely to feel safe and willing to take part in the beneficial aspects of the inpatient program.

Ensuring Emotional Safety. Experiences of sexual and physical abuse not only violate one's sense of physical safety but also damage one's emotional well-being. Trauma survivors may come to feel vulnerable in situations that might seem unthreatening under normal circumstances. Everyday sights, smells, and sounds may trigger painful memories that take a trauma survivor back to an experience of abuse. In a strange environment, like a hospital, where the trauma survivor feels out of control and unfamiliar with the rules and expectations, emotional safety is especially compromised. This paradoxical effect of an inpatient stay requires special attention since the intent of a hospitalization is to restore emotional equilibrium and balance. Achieving calm becomes difficult for some consumers who feel vulnerable and intimidated by the hospital environment. There are, however, several actions that staff can take to minimize the unsettling effect of a hospitalization:

• *Keeping consumers fully informed.* One of the most upsetting aspects of health care for consumers in general and for survivors of trauma in particular is not being fully informed. Staff should explain ward rules and procedures, but they should also take care to talk consumers through activities in advance of doing them. For example, if a woman is to be interviewed by a social worker, someone should explain to her in advance the nature of the interview, the length of the process, and how she can signal to the worker if she is unable to continue the session.

Daily ward activities, such as meals, provisions for personal hygiene, and any group or treatment activities the consumer is expected to attend, should be outlined in detail. It is often useful to have the same information presented in a variety of formats. A staff member, a peer counselor, and a written brochure may all present the same information. Staff need to be mindful that consumers who are frightened and overwhelmed may have difficulty processing even the most basic information. Some trauma survivors may find that they dissociate when simple rules are being explained. Consequently, it is helpful to have the same information available again and again in nonthreatening and nonshaming ways.

For many survivors of trauma, confusion was a reasonable response to the madness going on around them. As adults, those same trauma survivors may find that they once again feel confused whenever they are emotionally overwhelmed. Ward staff may find that when a consumer begins to feel emotionally safe, that person may be able to understand the same rules and expectations that confused him or her just a short time before. Staff should therefore not assume that when a trauma survivor reports feeling confused, she is describing a purely intellectual phenomenon. She may well be referring to her sense of emotional dis-ease and may need to be reassured rather than instructed to read the ward rules yet another time.

• *Identifying emotional triggers.* One of the most frightening aspects of needing a hospitalization is not being able to identify the triggers that led to feeling so out of control. For many men and women, especially if they have been discouraged over the years from paying attention to their own feelings and intuitions, the occasion of a hospitalization may feel like something that happened out of the blue. The consumer feels not only baffled but also helpless and frightened. He or she may recall feeling at the mercy of a powerful abuser and may now feel similarly overpowered by internal feelings and responses that seem to come from nowhere.

In every trauma-informed inpatient stay, the consumer should be assisted in developing a personal inventory of feelings, events, interpersonal situations, sights, sounds, and smells that might trigger feelings of being out of control or overwhelmed. An inventory begins with the realization that triggers may take many forms. For some, a particular feeling begins the cycle of losing control. For others, it may be an interpersonal dynamic such as being criticized or judged. For still others, it may be a physical sensation such as being touched in a sensitive spot or entering a room that is too small for comfort.

Identifying and learning to recognize emotional triggers restores a sense of emotional safety. The trauma survivor no longer need feel that tragic things just happen. She can come to appreciate that certain behaviors and feelings lead to other behaviors and feelings, and she can begin to develop a plan for gaining a sense of control and order in her life. When we feel that we can anticipate and control events, we no longer feel quite so vulnerable.

When control is restored solely by interventions done to you, the trauma survivor may feel better in the short term, but she does not leave the hospital with a sense that she will be better equipped to handle feeling out of control the next time that some feeling or behavior triggers an overwhelming response. Linehan (1993), in her work on dialectical behavior therapy, talked about the development of the "wise mind," a state of consciousness that uses what we know emotionally with what we know logically. The "wise mind" is engaged when we learn to recognize triggers and proceed with confidence to minimize their impact.

• *Identifying and developing soothing behaviors.* After consumers learn to recognize the triggers that precede feeling out of control, they must learn how to restore control if a crisis occurs. For some trauma survivors, it may seem novel to consider that there are simple ways to restore control. The feelings during a crisis are so overwhelming that a trauma survivor may overlook everyday strategies that can be used to restore equilibrium. Consumers feel a sense of emotional safety when they know that they possess the tools to comfort themselves and regain control.

As part of a trauma-informed inpatient stay, each consumer should have the opportunity to complete an assessment designed to help her identify the strategies that contribute to feeling comforted and in control. A complete assessment should include the activities that a trauma survivor can do on her own, such as writing in a journal or taking a warm bath, as well as activities that require another person, such as talking to a friend or having someone give her a hug. Strategies should also include distractors, such as counting to fifty or watching television, and techniques that bring bodily comfort.

Many men and women who are the survivors of abuse are reluctant to use strategies that involve their bodies. Consumers need to be invited to reconsider simple sources of bodily comfort. Self-massage, bathing, wrapping up in a warm blanket, using a cool washcloth on the face, and exercise are all ways that a consumer can soothe herself during times of stress. Similarly, in just a few hours, consumers can learn relaxation and deep breathing exercises that restore calm and can be used in almost any setting.

The more that consumers feel that they have tools for feeling good on their own, the more they feel safe with their own emotions. One of the more troubling experiences for any trauma survivor is to live in terror of feelings that well up unexpectedly. The consumer then feels both frightened of threats from the outside world and vulnerable to internal turmoil. Learning to comfort oneself gives a consumer a measure of emotional security that he or she may not have had prior to a trauma-informed hospitalization.

• *Having clear provisions for responding to accusations of abuse.* Despite the best precautions of staff and consumers, there are times when abuse occurs during an inpatient stay. The perpetrator may be another consumer, a visitor to the ward, or a staff member. Every treatment unit should have a set of policies and procedures in place for how to address accusations of abuse. The time for developing such policies is not when the first accusation is made.

Accusations should always be taken seriously. For many survivors, one of the most upsetting aspects of early trauma is that no one believed their reports of what was being done to them. Believing the consumer and making it safe for him or her to come forward is an important part of living the values of a trauma-informed program.

An outside committee that includes consumer-survivor members should conduct all investigations. Administrators should not assume that staff members, no matter how professional, could conduct an investigation on themselves. All inquiries should be conducted as soon as possible after the event and should be concluded quickly, with the resolution made public to all ward residents and staff. Appropriate resolution might include the initiation of legal action, termination of employment, or placement of a consumer on a different inpatient ward.

The safety, physical and emotional, of the consumer who is making the accusations should be guaranteed. She should receive extra support from counselors or peers and should experience no reprisal for having come forward. Many trauma survivors grow up fearing that things will "be worse if they tell." In a trauma-informed setting, the experience of coming forward should be as easy and nonshaming as possible.

Designing an Ideal Inpatient Unit

An ideal inpatient program provides the essentials of what psychiatrist and author Sandra Bloom (1997) calls "sanctuary." To provide sanctuary, comfort, and rest from turmoil, a unit must be informed by an understanding of trauma and the impact that violence of all types has on the lives of men and women. Respect for and collaboration with the consumer and his or her chosen helpers should inform all aspects of the inpatient stay.

Staff members should be trained in an understanding of trauma dynamics and should evidence a commitment to avoid interactions that retraumatize the consumer. Ward policies and procedures should be in the service of providing physical and emotional safety for the duration of a consumer's stay in the hospital. All staff working on the unit, from the psychiatrist to the maintenance workers, should receive basic training about trauma and its impact, and only staff who express an interest in being on the ward should be there. On a unit that will serve men and women who are the survivors of trauma, only those who want to be part of the treatment effort should be present.

Under most circumstances, inpatient stays tend to be relatively short. Consequently, intensive work in trauma recovery should be introduced but not forced or mandated. Generally the majority of recovery work occurs once a consumer leaves the hospital. On the unit, however, certain themes should be introduced to all consumers. A basic education about abuse and the impact it has on the lives of men and women should be made available. That information can come in the form of conversations with peer counselors, it can be part of psychoeducational training provided by ward staff, or it can be made available in the form of an informational film, such as *Women Speak Out* (Community Connections, 1999).

In addition, information should be provided to help consumers see the connections between current symptoms and traumatic events and to understand the triggers that may have precipitated the current hospitalization and the feelings that led to it. The goal of such psychoeducational presentations should be to help consumers gain an appreciation that behaviors are understandable and, moreover, that every example of symptomatic behavior contains an attempt to cope and to survive.

Finally, an inpatient stay should leave a consumer better able to manage his or her feelings than before the hospitalization occurred. First, by identifying and teaching strategies for self-soothing and symptom management, staff can assist consumers in beginning to acquire a sense of mastery and personal control. Although such teaching on the ward is important, it will rarely be sufficient to give consumers sufficient confidence to handle future crises. Therefore, an inpatient stay should end with a discussion of what to do next. Consumers who want referrals for follow-up care should be given a range of options, from traditional to alternative approaches for services. Consumers should also be assisted in developing a Wellness Recovery Action Plan while they are still on the ward and away from the demands of their everyday lives.

And finally, on an ideal unit, consumers should be allowed to get what help they can without being made to feel guilty for not using the hospital the way someone else feels they should. Recovery from the impact of abuse is a journey that takes each trauma survivor down an individual path. Each trauma survivor uses the resources available the best she can at the time and should not be made to feel inadequate or ashamed. Too many consumers leave hospitals feeling that they failed to do what they were supposed to do to get well.

Such shaming not only renders whatever was learned in the hospital useless, but also may make returning to the ward at another time almost impossible.

Avoiding Retraumatizing Practices

There are some obvious and other not so obvious practices that may leave consumers feeling traumatized by their inpatient experience. The use of physical restraints and locked seclusion rooms are examples of treatment interventions that consumers find "humiliating, depressing, and punishing" (Soliday, 1985). For consumers who have had experiences of sexual or physical abuse, these procedures may be all too reminiscent of tactics used by perpetrators in the past; therefore, rather than producing the desired effect of calming trauma survivors, they may trigger a flashback to a prior trauma. Even when there is not a history of prior abuse, having one's arms and legs tied down can be terrifying and feel like a violation.

A number of states have convened task forces to explore the use of these restrictive practices and to make recommendations on their use (Carmen and others, 1996). In general, the recommendations focus on how to use alternative strategies for calming consumers so that restraints are used as infrequently as possible. Restraint-reduction practices include a range of deescalation alternatives such as those already discussed. Recommendations also include suggestions for how to use restraints in the most humane way should they be needed. Avoiding a spread-eagle position, for example, is one such suggestion, as is the recommendation that consumers be given the option of having a same-sex staff person present during the procedure.

While seclusion and restraint are obvious examples of practices that may be experienced as traumatizing by consumers, there are many more subtle examples as well. Ann Jennings (1997), in her discussion of her daughter Anna's seventeen years of experience in the mental health system, outlines some of these:

- Being stripped of clothing in front of male attendants and being forcibly injected with medications in the buttocks
- Having intense feelings, especially of rage, suppressed and labeled as pathological
- Having reports of abuse disbelieved by staff
- Having relationships disrupted because of shift changes and other administrative reassignments
- Feeling that all of the control over one's well-being was in the hands of others
- Having one's responses to situations, minimized, discredited, or ignored

In order to avoid repeating trauma dynamics, inpatient staff must be given the opportunity to learn about abuse and the many ways that it shapes a trauma survivor's experience and, ultimately, worldview.

Conclusion

In a fully trauma-informed system, the need for inpatient hospitalization is kept to a minimum. Consumers and providers are aware of and employ alternative methods so that crises can be resolved in a trauma survivor's own home or a community facility. When hospitalizations are needed, programs should be designed to guarantee the physical and emotional safety of the consumer. And under no circumstances should the hospitalization be an experience of retraumatization for the consumer.

References

Bloom, S. *Creating Sanctuary*. New York: Routledge, 1997.

Carmen, E., and others. *Task Force on the Restraint and Seclusion of Persons Who Have Been Physically or Sexually Abused*. Boston: Massachusetts Department of Mental Health, 1996.

Community Connections. *Women Speak Out*. Washington, D.C.: Community Connections, 1999. Videotape.

Copeland, M. E. *WRAP: Wellness Recovery Action Plan*. Brattleboro, Vt.: Peach Press, 1997.

Freeman, D., and Fallot, R. "Trauma and Trauma Recovery for Dually Diagnosed Male Survivors." In M. Harris and C. Landis (eds.), *Sexual Abuse in the Lives of Women Diagnosed with Serious Mental Illness*. Amsterdam: Harwood Academic Publishers, 1997.

Jennings, A. "On Being Invisible in the Mental Health System." In M. Harris and C. Landis (eds.), *Sexual Abuse in the Lives of Women Diagnosed with Serious Mental Illness*. Amsterdam: Harwood Academic Publishers, 1997.

Linehan, M. *Cognitive-Behavioral Treatment of Borderline Personality Disorder*. New York: Guilford Press, 1993.

Soliday, S. "A Comparison of Patient and Staff Attitudes Toward Seclusion." *Journal of Nervous and Mental Disease,* 1985, *173*(5), 282–286.

Visalli, H., McNasser, G., Johnstone, L., and Lazzaro, C. "Reducing High Risk Interventions for Managing Aggression in Psychiatric Settings." *Journal of Quality Nursing Care,* 1997, *11,* 54–61.

Wile, J. "Inpatient Treatment of Psychiatric Women Patients with Trauma." In M. Harris and C. Landis (eds.), *Sexual Abuse in the Lives of Women Diagnosed with Serious Mental Illness*. Amsterdam: Harwood Academic Publishers, 1997.

MAXINE HARRIS is codirector of Community Connections in Washington, D.C., and executive director of its National Capital Center for Trauma Recovery and Empowerment.

ROGER D. FALLOT is codirector of Community Connections.

Supportive housing providers can play a vital role in the recovery of persons exposed to abuse and violence. Specific modifications for delivering housing support services are recommended based on an emerging trauma-informed perspective.

Trauma-Informed Approaches to Housing

Richard R. Bebout

Individuals diagnosed with mental illness and who have been exposed to traumatic violence throughout their lives are often unable to establish and maintain safe, stable housing without comprehensive supports. As a result, they are especially vulnerable to recurrent housing loss. Recognizing how the after-effects of trauma have contributed to residential instability, reframing these problematic behaviors as coping strategies, and promoting the development and application of new self-management skills in the housing environment represent unique opportunities, and indeed responsibilities, for supportive housing providers.

The housing arena can be a highly charged one for several reasons. First, many symptoms and behaviors associated with trauma go undetected in the office or clinic and are instead first recognized in residential settings. Second, abuse often happened initially in a trauma survivor's childhood home or in the home of a trusted caregiver; thus, the experience of "home" and expectations for home life are forever colored by the abuse experience. Third, many structural characteristics of the relationship between a resident in a supervised setting and a residential counselor have the potential to replicate key elements of abusive relationships: abuse happens when there is the opportunity for a trusted caregiver to be alone with the victim so that the abuse can go unnoticed by others; it happens in the context of a hierarchy in which one or more parties have power and control (real or perceived) over another who feels helpless to change or escape the situation; and it is compounded when the victim's cries are unheard, experience is denied, and the victim has no recourse. Fourth, exposure to abuses in institutional settings is also common and inevitably shapes the individual's expectations and responses to various residential settings.

On the other hand, residential settings that are genuinely trauma informed provide unique opportunities to acquire and practice new self-management skills, manage emotional and physical boundaries more effectively, and develop new social skills and strategies for dealing with close relationships. For all these reasons, extreme care must be taken to prevent abuses in residential settings and to establish policies and practices that reflect a sophisticated understanding of abuse dynamics and the process of recovery.

Trauma-Related Behaviors Frequently Manifested in the Housing Arena

Housing staff may benefit from understanding the role trauma may play in specific behaviors often encountered in residential settings.

Sleep Disturbances. Sleep disturbances are among the most prevalent after-effects of violence and abuse. Acute sleep difficulties such as extreme insomnia or night terrors are readily recognized as part of a posttraumatic stress response, but there are many other behaviors related to sleep that stem from trauma and abuse, as some examples show:

• A woman who had been sexually abused beginning at age nine could relax enough to fall asleep only if she remained fully clothed and slept on top of the covers with the lights on. Another woman was often found sleeping in the hallway. These patterns mystified and frustrated residential counselors until a supervisor suggested that both might have achieved some success in fending off their abusers or in attracting the attention of other childhood caregivers by adopting these strategies.

• A woman repeatedly slept on the couch in the television room, ostensibly because the air-conditioning in her bedroom was not working properly. Staff started to pressure her to return to her room after the outside temperatures dropped, only to have the resident produce a different rationalization for continuing to sleep on the couch. A clinical supervisor speculated that this was a carryover from an extensive history of physical abuse that left the woman feeling safer in public spaces in the group residence, although the resident herself may not have understood this connection.

• A woman in a supported apartment rarely slept at night, and her anxiety and agitation led her to place many calls to the agency's after-hours on-call service. This woman often slept through the day, thus making it difficult for her to keep appointments at the clinic or to maintain employment, although her skills were adequate and she was able to obtain jobs easily. Eventually this day-night reversal was attributed to her having been sexually abused in her childhood bedroom by an older male relative.

Self-Soothing Deficits. Trauma survivors' difficulties with self-soothing sometimes lead to behaviors that present special problems for supportive housing providers, such as addictive and other compulsive behaviors. Drinking and other forms of substance abuse sometimes arise out of the individual's efforts to cope with high levels of anxiety and arousal, but alcohol or other drug use frequently leads to expulsion from housing. Similarly, excessive smoking secondary to anxiety may lead to problems in mental health housing. Smoking is poorly tolerated inside many group home settings and may be dangerous in both supervised and independent living arrangements due to the risk of fire from smoking in bed or disposing of hot ashes improperly.

Privacy Needs and Boundary Issues. The prevalence of traumatic violence in the lives of mental health consumers living in specialized housing requires special attention to a range of boundary issues. These include personal space and physical boundaries, rules regarding nudity and dress in any kind of shared housing, privacy needs in bedrooms and bathrooms to promote and support healthy self-care, privacy for normal adult sexual activity, private space for telephone use and for visiting with guests, and the need for quiet space other than one's bedroom. These issues are highly sensitive and highly charged, particularly in the context of trauma recovery. Nudity, for example, may need to be prohibited because it can be upsetting, and even retraumatizing, for others, but the rules should be presented and enforced in ways that are not shaming.

Residential counselors have often worked and trained in institutional settings where risk management and safety concerns are given priority over personal privacy and dignity. Whereas staff in institutional settings may need to keep an acutely ill patient in their line of sight twenty-four hours a day, a consumer-resident in mental health housing should be encouraged to close doors with the expectation that such boundaries will be honored. A trauma survivor may initially fail to attend to his or her own boundaries and privacy needs, leaving bedroom and bathroom doors open. Similarly, a shut door may be completely ignored by a trauma survivor. Residential counselors, especially those with prior experience in institutional settings, must first change their own mind-set when working in a home environment rather than on a unit and should be encouraged to model and reinforce the practice of establishing and observing other people's boundaries and privacy rights.

Group living also creates opportunities to help residents change their relationship to their own bodies. Persons recovering from traumatic violence often have poor or unusual personal hygiene and bathroom habits: some neglect themselves rather dramatically, while others pay what some might consider excessive attention to their personal hygiene. One trauma survivor may cope with fears of revictimization by making herself unpleasant to be near, cultivating a body odor or deliberately being overweight, ill kempt, or unattractively dressed. Another may have an extreme preoccupation with cleanliness. A resident who takes frequent or long showers may be surprised to encounter tensions with housemates because the bathroom is tied up or the hot water is used up. Sensitizing residential counselors to these issues can help to reduce rigidity and allow them to intervene more respectfully when necessary.

Eating Problems. Eating disorders are common sequelae of abuse, especially emotional abuse. Trauma survivors living in mental health housing may exhibit a number of peculiar eating habits. For example, one woman was unable to eat in the presence of anyone else, and her case manager had to negotiate a special arrangement with the board-and-care provider to allow her to take a tray to her bedroom to eat. A man expressed frankly delusional ideas about his food being poisoned. Although both behaviors were read initially as simply psychotic, both were rooted in extensive emotional abuse in childhood. Those who have grown up with controlling and critical parents sometimes exhibit eating problems, including undereating, outright refusal to eat, extreme pickiness, or an inadequate diet. These behaviors often lead to misguided attempts by residential staff to enter into power struggles around food intake. Bingeing, compulsive overeating, and emotional eating to cope with profound feelings of emptiness, loneliness, depression, agitation, or other forms of distress are also common. For example, a morbidly obese woman raided the refrigerator in her group home almost nightly and added large amounts of butter to almost every food she consumed. Staff worked to limit her food intake and use of butter and to help her develop other ways of coping with upsetting feelings and mood states. Doing so without becoming controlling or even punitive is a tall order for residential counselors.

Extreme Behaviors. Self-injurious behavior such as cutting, intentionally self-inflicted cigarette burns, or head banging may first become apparent in a residential setting because the individual is less able to hide such behavior from staff or roommates. These behaviors almost universally emerge originally as attempts to cope with severe abuse and can be longstanding and quite resistant to change. They often escape the attention of clinicians for years until or unless the individual spends time in a controlled environment such as a hospital or supervised residential setting. Specialized mental health housing may be helpful in breaking the cycle of self-injury if the individual can be assisted in developing new coping and self-soothing strategies. On the other hand, self-injury can be exceptionally disturbing for the uninitiated, so that both staff and peers react very intensely. As a result, sometimes the behavior simply goes underground rather than getting worked with constructively. Careful training and supervision are needed to allow residential counselors to intervene helpfully and to have realistic expectations about changing these entrenched self-destructive behaviors.

Patterns of Sexual Adjustment. Survivors of sexual abuse can have great difficulty making a reasonably healthy sexual adjustment. Some are prone to sexualizing relationships inappropriately because sexual give and take has been the prevailing currency in most relationships. Some survivors become hypersexual, some vigorously avoid any sexual contact, and many others alternate between extremes. Housing providers can expect to see all of the patterns of sexual relating and must find ways to assist residents in both congregate and independent settings to make safe and informed choices for themselves. Too often staff in residential programs operate as if residents are completely nonsexual or believe the program can prohibit sexual activity. Instead, residential service providers need to strive to establish frank dialogue with residents regarding their intimate relationships, including those that involve sex. In congregate housing, ongoing sexual relationships within a residence can be problematic because of the lack of privacy and because of the impact on other residents. Couplings within a residence can be disorganizing for both members of the couple as well as others, tensions and jealousies can occur, and pressure to maintain secrecy may arise. Some survivors may be retraumatized by sexual activity by peers within the group home, making it difficult or impossible to meet everyone's needs. The need to monitor and intervene when relationships develop exists alongside the need to model healthy attitudes about mutually satisfying and respectful adult sexual relationships.

Avoiding Retraumatization in Mental Health Housing

Factors such as the power differential between staff and consumers in mental health housing can replicate structural aspects of past abusive relationships. Because housing providers, especially live-in residential counselors, control a critical resource—access to housing—residents may become intimidated easily, feel unable to assert their needs and rights, and fear loss of housing. This element may evoke fears of earlier abusive relationships in which a powerful adult may have directly or indirectly threatened to harm the abuse victim or to withhold needed assistance, tangible or intangible. Housing providers must understand how real this threat is to a vulnerable consumer.

Another scenario that recalls aspects of earlier abuses is the spoken or implied request that the powerless individual hold secrets. In mental health housing, counselors sometimes receive visits from friends or family members, even overnight, a clear violation of the rules in most systems. Or a counselor may decide to leave the residence unattended, perhaps for hours, again without permission and without making appropriate provisions for the residents. This neglect is reminiscent of the absentee parent who leaves the emotionally abused child to fend for himself for extended periods; this is compounded by the parent's insistence that this remain "our little secret."

Actual abuses—emotional, physical, and sexual—happen more regularly in housing programs than anyone wants to admit. These range from yelling, name calling, critical comments, and put-downs to preferential treatment, flirting and sexual innuendo, inappropriate touching, physical aggression, and frank sexual contact. Special relationships can develop between residents and counselors living together around the clock in a

homelike setting, counselors can become overly involved and overly identified with residents, counselors may disclose more about themselves in
housing settings than in an office environment, and it is more difficult in
general to establish and maintain adequate professional distance. Often residential counselors have less training and supervision and more direct contact with consumers than any other member of the treatment team. Housing
systems must take active steps to protect consumers from subtle and not-
so-subtle abuses through prevention activities like training and supervision.
Programs should also implement and publicize zero-tolerance policies that
prohibit the abuse of mental health consumers and provide for swift and
decisive action against violators.

Toward a Trauma-Informed Approach to Housing

Housing services should be guided by the principles of safety, self-
determination, empowerment, self-management, predictability, choice, and
collaborative decision making. These are consistent with the philosophy
espoused by supported housing advocates (Carling, 1993) and by the consumer movement evident in mental health reforms today. A trauma perspective further sensitizes us to ways that specific practices can advance or erode
progress toward recovery for individual trauma survivors (Harris, 1994). The
following modifications represent key steps toward a trauma-informed
approach to housing supports.

Trauma-Informed Housing Assessment. Prevalence data indicate
that trauma is virtually universal among dually diagnosed women who have
been homeless (Goodman, Dutton, and Harris, 1995). Trauma may be
linked to homelessness and residential instability in a variety of ways. Supportive housing staff should work closely with a prospective resident and
her team to construct a careful housing history. Where tolerated, the history
should seek to establish possible links between a seemingly random series
of unrelated residential moves and the after-effects of trauma. Bringing such
a trauma perspective to understanding one's housing history and current
housing support needs can serve to render the chaos in the trauma survivor's life more understandable. As patterns of instability become more
comprehensible, the trauma survivor begins to feel new hope about getting
his or her life under control.

Maximizing Choice. A trauma-informed perspective underscores the
importance of providing consumer-survivors with a range of suitable options
and working collaboratively with an individual to design a viable support
plan. Housing placements or assignments cannot be based solely on availability or administrative ease. Instead, to the maximum extent possible, consumers must be shown a range of housing options from which to choose.

Respecting Privacy Needs, Promoting Healthy Boundaries. All adults
need privacy, and abuse survivors in mental health housing may have great
privacy needs because their boundaries have often been violated throughout

their lives. They may in fact not even recognize or have any capacity to assert their own needs for personal space. Whenever consumers live with others, private bedrooms are a must. Adult trauma survivors should not be asked to share bedrooms. Bathroom and bedroom doors should be outfitted with privacy locks whenever feasible. Residential counselors must knock on doors and wait for the resident to respond. Even if a resident is thought to be a danger to herself in some way, making it necessary for staff to conduct a room check for the individual's own safety, staff should not simply ignore a closed door. A bedroom at home is not the same as a hospital room.

Advance Directives. At a minimum, advance directives for housing should encompass the following factors:

- Include the names of individuals within the residence and contact persons outside the residence with whom the individual feels particularly safe.
- Identify specific containment strategies, language, and staff behaviors that are particularly helpful in deescalating the resident.
- Name things such as language, nonverbal cues, rooms in the house, physical touch, or other behaviors that are likely to trigger feelings of panic or lead to dissociation.
- Specify a doctor and a hospital or alternative, such as a crisis house or the home of a trusted family member or friend, where the person might go if feeling out of control.

Adaptive Self-Soothing. Coupled with advance directives, residents should be encouraged to develop, review, and practice a variety of self-soothing strategies. Residents should be encouraged to record their own unique self-soothing strategies on a "comfort card." If the consumer chooses to share her comfort card with residential staff, counselors can familiarize themselves with each resident's list and encourage her to use those strategies as needed. The following actions can also promote the development of new and adaptive self-soothing in residential settings:

- Provide quiet space in addition to a bedroom where a resident can be alone for a brief time to read or pursue some other self-soothing strategy.
- Make music and stereo equipment available.
- Have exercise equipment available.
- Encourage residents to use perfumes or other scents that they find calming or grounding.
- Stock healthy snacks, and encourage moderate use of "comfort foods" of the resident's own choosing.

Staff Training and Supervision. Residential staff should be given a general overview of trauma, its various forms, and common after-effects. Counselors should also be introduced to the notion that symptomatic behavior often arises out of the trauma survivor's efforts to cope with unbearable circumstances. Staff training and supervision must also include explicit guidelines prohibiting most forms of physical touching and should address other boundary issues as well, such as respecting closed doors. Perhaps hardest of all for former hospital employees, staff working in mental health housing should work to set a collaborative tone rather than an authoritarian one.

Single-Sex Housing. Some individuals may need the option of an all-female or all-male group home or apartment building in order to feel safe. Staff of the same sex may also be necessary in staffed residences.

Clear Statement of Program Rules and Expectations. If housing settings are to be safe and predictable, residents should be provided with clear, written program statements that set out what is expected of them and what they can expect from staff. Staff should always tell a resident what they are doing before they do it, such as conducting a room inspection or admitting a new resident. When staff members plan to take time off, they should tell the residents in advance and identify their replacement by name, if possible, so a resident will not be surprised on awakening in the morning or returning home in the afternoon. Many trauma survivors experienced chaotic home environments, waking up to find strangers in their homes or not knowing where they were or where parents were.

Collaborative Decision Making. To the maximum extent possible, consumers must be full partners in determining the following:

- Where to live (neighborhood, access to transportation, amenities, and so forth)
- What level of supervision and tangible support they need
- With whom they will live—that is, alone or with a roommate they choose
- How often, and even whether, to have regular home visits versus office-based visits from case managers
- When moves will occur
- Which risks to take, balancing liability concerns with the individual's need for and right to self-determination within broad limits bounded only by safety considerations

Conclusion

Trauma survivors experience repeated disruptions in their housing, have difficulty maintaining even minimally safe conditions in their own housing once they obtain it, and find themselves perpetually in harm's way when cycling between marginal housing arrangements and homelessness. Trauma survivors seeking supportive housing services present special challenges. However, service planners and providers working to meet the housing needs of mental health consumers are uniquely positioned to facilitate the recovery process of abuse survivors. Housing settings that are genuinely trauma informed offer trauma survivors the opportunity to acquire and practice new self-management and relationship skills and to experience "home" in new ways.

References

Carling, P. J. "Housing and Supports for Persons with Mental Illness: Emerging Approaches to Research and Practice." *Hospital and Community Psychiatry,* 1993, *44,* 439–449.

Goodman, L. A., Dutton, M. A, and Harris, M. "Physical and Sexual Assault Prevalence Among Episodically Homeless Women with Serious Mental Illness." *American Journal of Orthopsychiatry,* 1995, *65*(4), 468–478.

Harris, M. "Modifications in Service Delivery and Clinical Treatment for Women Diagnosed with Severe Mental Illness Who Are Also the Survivors of Sexual Abuse Trauma." *Journal of Mental Health Administration,* 1994, *21*(4), 397–406.

RICHARD R. BEBOUT is clinical housing director at Community Connections in Washington, D.C.

*Because addictive disorders are so common among women
who have experienced prolonged sexual and physical
abuse, it is especially important to design addictions
services that meet the needs of the trauma survivor.*

Designing Trauma-Informed Addictions Services

Maxine Harris, Roger D. Fallot

In all areas of service delivery, trauma-informed services should take into account the particular needs and special requirements of the consumer. In some areas, that means that services should be gender specific. Within the addictions field in particular, treatments have often been designed with male consumers in mind (Drabble, 1996). Therefore, to be truly trauma informed, addictions services must be redesigned with female consumers and their needs at the center of program development efforts. Many of the principles outlined in this chapter may also be applicable to male consumers of addictions services, but the programmatic suggestions derive from the special needs of women in treatment.

Integrating Trauma and Addictions Services

Trauma-informed addictions services are also integrated services; that is, the symptoms of trauma and the consequences of addiction are addressed within a single system and by a single model of care. In keeping with trauma-informed principles, an integrated approach addresses the needs of the whole person and is based on the assumption that the problems of substance abuse and trauma interact in a complex way within the life and the psyche of a single individual. The two sets of problems are addressed simultaneously by strategies that focus on common issues, present integrative explanations, and teach comprehensive skills (Evans and Sullivan, 1995).

An integrated approach exists in contrast to both parallel and sequential treatment options and avoids some of the pitfalls of these alternative approaches. In a parallel treatment model, a woman receives separate trauma and addictions services simultaneously at the hands of two distinct sets of providers. Each provider is trained and committed to addressing only one set of problems. The addictions program deals with problems related to chemical dependency, while the trauma program addresses the sequelae of abuse. In the parallel treatment model, there is often a lack of coordination among various providers, and the messages delivered by different caregivers may be conflicting or even contradictory. For example, a substance abuse program may require that a consumer abstain from all drugs, even those prescribed by a physician. A trauma program, in contrast, may recommend that a woman take medication to help calm her anxiety while she is dealing with her abuse issues.

Beyond the lack of coordination, a parallel model perpetuates the notion that problems and parts of the self can be compartmentalized and dealt with separately. The dual treatment approach acts as if each problem belongs to a separate person and exists independent of all the other aspects of an individual's life. Regrettably, a parallel approach to treatment runs the risk of replicating the compartmentalization that may already exist in a trauma survivor's way of coping with her abuse in the past or present. Many trauma survivors find that the only way they can manage the overwhelming impact of abuse is to view the abuse as if it exists in a parallel universe and has nothing to do with their "real lives."

Consumers encounter different, but no less significant, problems when trauma and addictions services operate within a sequential treatment model. In this model, providers assume that treatment for chemical dependency should be completed, or at least be well underway, before any trauma treatment can begin. The addictions intervention can consist of inpatient detoxification or treatment programs, residential group homes or halfway houses, outpatient day hospital or therapy groups, or self-help Narcotics Anonymous or Alcoholics Anonymous meetings. Regardless of the format, however, the addictions treatment always precedes the trauma treatment in a sequential approach.

This sequencing is based on two separate assumptions. First, the addictive disorder is assumed to be the primary problem and thus in need of attention before any other issues, which are regarded as secondary, are addressed. This is a core belief that the provider community holds. The consumer herself may view her abuse issues as primary, but the treatment system maintains a commitment to addressing the chemical dependency issues before any other concerns are even considered. In some cases, a consumer's preference for dealing with her trauma issues first will be seen as a way of avoiding her substance abuse problem. Unfortunately, when providers tell consumers that they "know what is best for them," they run the risk of replicating abuse dynamics in which a perpetrator decided what was best independent of a woman's wishes and needs.

The second assumption of a sequential treatment model is that a consumer needs a clear and drug-free mind before she can begin to focus on her trauma issues. Although this assumption clearly makes sense, it harbors an underlying belief that trauma symptoms and addictive problems are not intertwined in complex ways. For example, many women report that they use substances as a way to manage overwhelming trauma symptoms, such as flashbacks or intrusive memories. If substances are removed as a coping option without some attention being paid to the underlying trauma symptoms, a woman may find that she is even less able to manage her trauma-related responses and behaviors. Paradoxically, she may feel even more compelled to use substances as a way of managing her reemerging trauma symptoms and may feel as if she has once again failed at being able to take care of herself in healthy ways.

Understanding the Links in an Integrated Trauma-Addictions Model

The fundamental assumption of a trauma-informed addictions system is that the connections between substance use and violent victimization in the lives of women seeking treatment for addictive disorders are both complex and varied. Treatment providers should assume that violence has played some role in the chemically dependent woman's life, whether she identifies abuse as a source of difficulty or not. That is not to suggest that the provider should force a trauma agenda, but rather that he or she should be aware of the pervasiveness of the links between violence and substance use. Those links are apparent in a survey of the relevant prevalence data, an appreciation of the histories of family violence that surround childhood abuse, an understanding of the ways in which drugs and alcohol are used to deal with the short- and long-term effects of abuse, and an awareness of the violence endemic in the culture of addictions.

Prevalence Data. Drug and alcohol use figure prominently in the lives of women who are survivors of sexual and physical abuse. A history of childhood sexual or physical abuse (or both) is considered to be a significant risk factor for the development of a substance use disorder (Evans and Sullivan, 1995). Studies of women in substance abuse treatment programs reveal that from 30 to 75 percent of women substance abusers have been victims of sexual abuse (Root, 1989). And although diverse interpretations have been offered to explain the connection between violent abuse and addiction, ranging from low self-esteem to a loss of important interpersonal connections, the very fact that a correlation seems to exist must be a part of any substance abuse recovery program. Finkelstein (1996) has noted that by acknowledging the connection between addiction and violence, providers validate a woman's experience and give her the strong message that she is not alone and that her experience is nothing of which she must be ashamed. When women feel that their violent abuse is unique, they feel alone and unable to benefit from the support and help of others. By being aware of and sharing relevant prevalence data, providers help to remove the sense of isolation and shame that so many survivors of abuse experience.

Family Histories of Violence. For many women, experiences of abuse were associated with the perpetrator's substance use. Evans and Sullivan (1995) report that a high correlation exists between parents, particularly fathers, having a substance abuse disorder and subsequent physical and sexual abuse directed toward their children. A National Crime Victimization Survey Report (Office of Justice Programs, Bureau of Justice Statistics, 1994) on violence against women revealed that in cases of sexual violence and rape, nearly 50 percent of the victims believed that their attacker was under the influence of drugs or alcohol at the time of the offense. More specifically, data reveal that 65 percent of incest offenders were drinking at the time of the abuse (Coleman, 1987). Another study uncovered that 57 percent of alcoholic women who had alcoholic fathers were incest survivors and had experienced repeated episodes of abuse over a long duration at the hands of fathers who were almost always drinking at the time of the sexual assault (Finkelstein, 1996).

The connection between the substance abuse of the perpetrator and the sexual and physical abuse of the victim is important for several reasons beyond the obvious identification of risk factors and early intervention aimed at prevention. For the survivor of violent abuse, drug and alcohol abuse and violence are forever linked. The trauma survivor may use the presence of the drug as a way to understand or excuse the abuser. She may see drugs, and not an abusive parent, as the culpable agent, leading her to mistake perpetrators for safe partners in the future. The trauma survivor may also come to see drugs as evil and to view all who use drugs or alcohol as bad people. This view is especially damaging to the woman who eventually uses substances herself, because she may then see herself as an evil woman undeserving of any type of help or concern. Circumstances become even more complicated if the perpetrator gave a young girl drugs or alcohol during the abuse to make her more compliant. She may then feel that she has no right to accuse her abuser and that she deserves a life of addiction and degradation.

Within a trauma-informed recovery program, providers can help women to see the legitimate connections between perpetrator substance use and violence and consequently to ascribe blame and responsibility accurately. Providers who hold to a genetic understanding of the transmission of alcoholism may want to wait until a trauma survivor has sufficiently distanced herself from an identification with her abuser before suggesting that the tendency to drink or use drugs was inherited from the abuser.

Using Substances to Manage the Impact of Abuse. A woman who has been sexually and physically abused has to contend with powerful emotions and interpersonal chaos. Regrettably, some women discover that they can ease the pain left by trauma by taking certain drugs or drinking alcohol. In a trauma-informed addictions program, women need to see the connections between the feelings they are trying to manage and the substances they choose to use and abuse. These explanations should not devolve into an "excuse for use" session, but they should help a woman to place her use in context and begin to consider alternative ways by which she might manage some of the more disturbing consequences of her history of violent abuse.

Following are some commonly presented trauma symptoms and the drugs women use to ease or manage them:

- *Depression.* Many women report feeling hopeless and despairing about their lives and their prospects for ever feeling good again. Drugs such as cocaine, which elevate mood even for a short time, may seem like a panacea to women who experience prolonged bouts of depression.
- *Anxiety.* Trauma leaves some women feeling anxious and fearful. In the short term, they may be worried that more abuse will be forthcoming, and in the long term they may experience a pervasive sense of dis-ease and worry. Alcohol and some tranquilizers such as the benzodiazepines can lessen the anxiety of a woman who feels chronically on edge.
- *Inner turmoil and pain.* Women who are plagued by flashbacks and recurring memories of the abuse may feel that the intensity of their experience is too great to bear. They may seek drugs that induce forgetting and tend to dull or numb all sensation. These women are at especially high risk for choosing opiates or alcohol to dull the pain.
- *The absence of all feeling.* While some women feel too much, others report that the abuse has left them unable to feel anything at all. They remark on the absence of all sensations, from sexual arousal to everyday feelings of happiness or sadness. For these women, any substance that produces an increase in sensation is appealing. They may find themselves drawn to cocaine or amphetamines for an immediate rush or to hallucinogens for a heightening of experience.
- *Passivity.* A long-term consequence of the abuse for some women is the absence of any motivation or any ability to stand up for themselves. They may report that they see no choice other than to submit when someone is aggressive or intimidating toward them, and they wish that they could feel legitimate anger or assertiveness. Drugs such as alcohol or PCP that release and enhance anger may have a particular appeal for women who believe that they are "too passive."
- *Excessive anger and rage.* When women acknowledge what was done to them at the hands of an abuser, they may experience overwhelming feelings of anger coupled with a desire for retaliation. If the abuser is no longer living or is inaccessible due to illness or distance, a woman may find that she feels angry but has no legitimate outlet for her rage. In some cases she will turn to drugs that leave her feeling less angry and more accepting or mellow. She may choose alcohol, marijuana, or opiates to inhibit her feelings of anger and indignation.
- *Sexual numbing.* It is not uncommon for women who have been sexually abused to report having no sexual feelings at all. Because they associate sex with the abuse, all sexual response may seem dangerous or dirty to them. Yet when they reach adolescence and seek to have romantic relationships, they

may feel defective if they are unable to respond sexually. Drugs such as alcohol, which serve to lessen inhibitions, or drugs that heighten sensation, such as amyl nitrate and some of the hallucinogens, might be tempting to a young woman who is trying to feel sexually alive.

• *Isolation and disconnection from others.* Experiences of sexual and physical abuse destroy one's sense of healthy connection to others. A girl feels isolated within her own family, with her peers, and in her community. Survivors of childhood abuse report feeling different from and estranged from their peers, leaving them alone and lonely at a time when social relationships are vital to defining a sense of self. For some young women, using drugs is the only way to feel part of a social group. When she is high, a young woman may finally feel that she is not only part of the group but that she is an acceptable member of society. Drugs give her a focus for her relationships with others as well as help her to feel more relaxed and socially adept. The actual drug used may therefore be less important than the fact that other members of the group or a particular romantic partner use it. In fact, partner use has been found to be a significant factor in the drug use of young mothers (Amaro, Freed, Cabral, and Zuckerman, 1990).

• *Suicidality.* For some women, the pain left behind by abuse is so overwhelming that the only solution they see for their despair is suicide. For these women, drugs and alcohol become the vehicle for carrying out the suicidal wish. The overuse of almost any drug can be life threatening. Some women are explicit in their desire to die of an "accidental" overdose and continue using, waiting for fate to end their suffering.

By understanding the role that substances play in managing her trauma symptoms, a survivor takes several important steps in her recovery. First, she acknowledges that she suffers from painful feelings and troubled relationships. Then she comes to see that those feelings are the result of her abuse history. And finally she recognizes the connections between her current pattern of substance use and her attempts to manage her trauma symptoms. This recognition is a first important step toward learning new skills for managing those same symptoms without resorting to substance use, which then has its own devastating consequences.

The Culture of Addictions. Illegal drug use or the heavy use of alcohol puts a woman at high risk for additional abuse. The world of the addict is a dangerous one, with transactions taking place at odd hours, in dangerous neighborhoods, and with often ruthless dealers. Women who are using heavily, living on the streets, or crashing with drug-using acquaintances encounter desperate and dangerous peers who may think nothing of committing violence to obtain drugs or money. In a study of dangerous behavior conducted at Community Connections in Washington, D.C., 30 percent of dually diagnosed women had experienced an episode of sexual or physical violence in the month prior to being interviewed for the study (Goodman, Dutton, and Harris, 1995).

Within the drug subculture, it is not uncommon for women to trade sex for money or directly for drugs. For survivors of sexual abuse, the act of obtaining drugs by using sex may then become a reenactment or a painful reminder of the earlier trauma. Women who trade sex are also subject to humiliation and degradation, often being called "tramp, lush, or whore" by everyone from customers to family members (Finkelstein, 1996). For a woman who may already feel that she is evil and unworthy, such name calling is only further corroboration that she deserves whatever bad treatment she might receive.

If a woman is using drugs or alcohol and selling sex to support herself, her chances of being raped are quite high. Moreover, substance-abusing women who are childhood abuse survivors are even more likely to be sexually abused as adults (Wallen and Berman, 1992). Paradoxically, however, despite the high incidence of sexual violence, many women either fail to identify the rape as a crime or to blame the attacker. Instead, they are inclined to blame themselves and their addictions for the sexual violence they experience. Some of the self-blame is in keeping with the trauma survivor's willingness to blame herself for anything that goes wrong. Some other part of the self-blame, however, may come from the recovering woman's growing awareness that using drugs and alcohol impaired her judgment and caused her to put herself in dangerous situations. As she progresses even further in her understanding of the connection between addiction and trauma, she may come to accept her own poor judgment while still holding an attacker culpable for his violent behavior.

Core Elements of a Trauma-Informed Addictions Program

Beyond the core assumption that there are multiple and complex connections between addictions and sexual and physical abuse trauma are several programmatic elements that need to be in place to make an addictions program fully trauma informed:

- The program must have a commitment to teaching explanations that integrate trauma and substance use.
- The milieu must promote consumer empowerment and relationship building as well as healing.
- Each woman must be encouraged to develop certain crossover skills that are equally important in recovery from trauma and chemical dependency.
- A series of ancillary services help a woman to continue her recovery once she leaves a structured program.
- The program avoids the use of recovery tactics that are contraindicated for women recovering from physical and sexual violence.

Teaching Integrative Explanations. Within a trauma-informed addictions program, consumers are exposed to contextual explanations that link substance use with histories of violence. These explanations are not intended to be excuses for why people use drugs, but rather are designed to place a woman's substance use in the context of her trauma history. The explanations, which follow, stress the role of triggers to use and the function of symptoms as self-soothing and coping strategies:

- Primary trauma is a stressor that may trigger substance use.
- Primary trauma is a stressor that may trigger the development of psychiatric symptoms or relationship patterns that may then trigger substance use.
- Symptoms that result from trauma such as flashbacks and nightmares are stressors that may trigger substance use.
- Substance use may have begun as an attempt to cope with primary trauma or the long-term effects of trauma.
- Substance use may persist as a way to self-soothe when trauma symptoms are especially troubling.

Integrative explanations give women a way to begin to make sense of their substance use. For some women, this will be the first time that they have considered any explanations at all. For others, these explanations will serve as alternatives to the medical model of addictive disorders. And for still others, these integrative explanations will not supplant biochemically based theories, but will merely add some complexity to how a woman understands her addiction. Because of the focus on triggers and self-soothing, these explanations suggest ways in which a woman might begin to change her behavior and start the process of recovery.

Establishing the Program Milieu. Programs must be based on strengths rather than deficits. Many trauma survivors begin programs believing that there is something profoundly wrong with them and that they can do nothing right or good. A program that inadvertently stresses the deficits that the chemically dependent woman has in managing her addiction serves only to reinforce her sense of inadequacy. When a woman's substance use itself is seen as an attempt to cope, she may begin to consider that even her most damaging behavior contained within it is an attempt to save herself from despair. Beyond emphasizing the coping inherent in the addictive behavior, trauma-informed programs must help consumers to reexamine all of their behaviors in terms of the strengths contained and perhaps hidden in complex behavior patterns. Such an examination also conveys to consumers that treatment providers believe that program participants have the capacity to succeed.

Programs should also emphasize the empowerment of each woman and of women in general. To that latter end, female staff members, women in recovery who can serve as sponsors or mentors, and a cadre of women in various stages of recovery should be available to serve as role models. It is important for women to believe that they have the power within themselves to move beyond the devastating impact of trauma and addictions.

Whenever possible, women should have as much control over their own recovery as they feel able to manage. This means that women should be able to choose some of the groups and classes that they will attend. They should also have some control over their personal space and their communal governance if they are in a residential program. Too often programs become invested in making women feel that they must prove themselves worthy of trust and autonomy rather than assuming that all women have within themselves the power to be responsible adults. Trauma-informed programs should therefore work to avoid a posture that says "guilty until proven innocent."

A trauma-informed approach should emphasize the importance of relationships in women's lives and capitalize on the importance that relationships have for women in general. Work on the psychology of women has highlighted the importance of relationships for all aspects of women's development (Jordan and others, 1991). Women not only define themselves by their important relationships, as mothers, daughters, and partners, but they derive much of their self-esteem from their important relationships and their ability to help and respond to the needs of others. Recovery programs that disparage close relationships as "codependent" and that encourage a self-first or a self-only approach fail to recognize how important relationships are in the lives of women.

Furthermore, the connections that women make with one another and with treatment providers are essential to recovery. Trauma-informed programs need to provide opportunities for women to bond together with one another and to form caring connections. This often happens when services are delivered in a group format, but there also need to be opportunities for informal sharing and connections. Similarly, consumers in addictions programs need the chance to form relationships with treatment staff, who may or may not also be persons in recovery. A trauma-informed program believes the feminist mantra that "women grow in connection."

An appreciation of the role of relationships in women's lives must extend beyond the confines of the treatment program. A woman's need to be with her children and to know that they are safe must be honored. Similarly, women in recovery should be able to continue to perform important relationship functions as friends, daughters, and siblings and should begin to learn how to balance those relationship demands with their own needs for quiet and solitude. Programs should be careful not to assume that if a woman attends to her family, she is necessarily running away from her own recovery.

Finally, programs should establish a milieu that is warm, friendly, and nurturing. Communal meals, the availability of nutritious snacks, and a well-lit and well-decorated environment give a woman the sense that her recovery matters and that she is a person worthy of care and respect. Staff members should be trained to treat all consumers with respect and warmth and to avoid tactics that are shaming or aggressively confrontational. The program should above all else be a safe place, where a woman feels that she can address her addictive behaviors without fear of further abuse.

Building Crossover Skills. The core of all trauma-informed addictions programs is the acquisition of skills that are independently and equally necessary for recovery and healing from chemical dependency and the aftermath of sexual and physical abuse. These crossover skills both allow a woman to make judgments in the future that avoid the damaging consequences of past violence and past substance abuse, and reinforce the all-important connection between trauma and addictive disorders. The core crossover skills include intrapersonal tools such as increasing self-knowledge, enhancing self-regulation, and self-soothing, and building self-esteem and self-trust, as well as interpersonal skills such as understanding limit setting and assertiveness, learning clear expression of needs and desires, mastering clear communication, perceiving others and situations clearly while applying accurate labels, and working toward mutuality and reciprocity in relationships.

Self-Knowledge. Experiences of sexual and physical abuse often distort what a woman knows to be true about her feelings and her responses. She may lose an awareness of her body in a need to protect herself from the pain of abuse. She may have difficulty distinguishing among thoughts, feelings, and actions that occurred in the past and those that are occurring now or might take place at some time in the future. Similarly, a woman abusing substances may be numbed to how she feels. She also may realize that denying how she feels has become a way of continuing to engage in behaviors that are dangerous and destructive. In either case, women must relearn, or learn for the first time, how to read the responses of their bodies accurately. They must be given tools for answering simple questions like, "How do you feel?" by learning to pay attention to bodily cues that they have long ignored.

Self-Regulation. Feeling out of control can be one of the triggers that lead women to use drugs and alcohol. Similarly, a trauma survivor's inability to control overwhelming feelings may lead to self-destructive relationships or behaviors and may be one of the pathways into the labyrinth of the mental health system for many trauma survivors. Understanding which events trigger overwhelming feelings and learning how to avoid them or contain their impact are essential recovery skills. Similarly, women benefit from learning how to express those feelings without feeling controlled by them. Repeated practice with limited expression, followed by a return to a place of calm and balance, helps women to believe that they can indeed control their affective expressions.

Self-Soothing. Often women know how to comfort themselves only in ways that are ultimately self-destructive. A woman may use drugs or alcohol, excessive overeating, or promiscuous sex as ways to gain comfort. Many women report being at a loss when asked to think of ways to gain comfort that might produce fewer risks. Herman (1992), among others, has noted that self-care is almost always disturbed among survivors of childhood sexual abuse. Women not only need to learn skills like relaxation, guided imaging, and journaling, but they need the opportunity to practice and feel comfortable with a new repertoire of self-soothing techniques.

Self-Esteem. Self-esteem and feelings of self-worth are deeply diminished in women who are abuse survivors and for women who abuse drugs and alcohol. Many women may be confused about just what self-esteem really is. They may know only that they harbor a profound sense of unhappiness about who they are. As part of a skill-building program, women need to realize that self-esteem is not an immutable trait; it is a state of mind that can vary across behaviors and over time. By realizing that they can alter the way they feel about themselves, women can begin to target specific behaviors that they want to change in order to raise their self-esteem.

Self-Trust. Often abusers attempt to be the arbiter of reality for the victim, telling her that he knows better than she does what is good for her and that her judgment is impaired and faulty. Many trauma survivors grow up assuming that their evaluations of things will be wrong. Similarly, women with long histories of substance use may have ample evidence that their judgment, especially when it comes to drug use, is inaccurate or distorted. Women need to begin with a careful assessment of what they know and how they know it, recognizing that their judgment may be good in one area and poor in another. As women begin to recognize multiple sources of data that should go into making any decision, they can decide which sources should weigh more heavily for particular decisions. Practice making decisions, followed by candid and constructive feedback, gives women the confidence that they can begin to trust their own judgments and also alerts them to areas for which they might want to seek backup advice.

Limit Setting and Assertiveness. Trauma survivors have had multiple experiences during which their personal boundaries were violated by a powerful abuser. Assertiveness in those circumstances might have jeopardized a woman's safety or even her life. Regrettably, many trauma survivors learn that limits are not theirs to set and consequently become oblivious to even the grossest violations of their personal boundaries. Similarly, women who have been involved in drug-seeking activities may have felt that the relinquishment of personal limits was the trade they needed to make in order to continue their supply of drugs. Women who have said yes so often in order to satisfy a drug craving may feel that they have forfeited the right to say no. As part of a skill-building program, women first need to recognize what their personal limits are across a variety of situations and then need practice in asserting and defending those limits.

Clear Expression of Needs and Desires. Because there was no one to listen or respond to what they needed or wanted, many trauma survivors learned that it was safer to need and want nothing. A trauma survivor may find herself looking for an ulterior motive when someone asks her what she wants and may refuse to offer even a tentative response. For women who have been addicted to drugs or alcohol, the only need they may have been willing to acknowledge was the need to use. Other needs or desires may have been forced into the background and long ago forgotten. Women need the opportunity to distinguish those things, both tangible and emotional, that they need from those that they want but could live without. They then need a mechanism for evaluating the reasonableness of those desires and a plan for how to achieve those that seem attainable.

Clear Communication. Many trauma survivors who tried to report ongoing abuse have learned that clear communication can get them into trouble; consequently, they have developed a skill for communicating through innuendo, nonverbal cues, and careful omissions of important information. Once women learn to identify what they need and want, they must practice effective techniques for communicating those desires clearly and unambiguously to others. Women also need to recognize that clear communication does not ensure that they will have their needs satisfied. Clarity ensures only that they will have made their needs known. Often women become angry because they imagine that if they finally learn to state what they want, they will be assured of success. They must realize that even with clear communication, their needs may not be met, and they need to develop both alternative strategies for getting their needs met and ways to deal with disappointment.

Accurate Perceptions of Others and Honest Labeling. In the worlds of both the trauma survivor and the substance user, emotional and physical survival may depend on *not* seeing people and situations for what they are. The drug addict could not possibly go into dangerous neighborhoods and do business with threatening dealers if she saw them clearly. Instead, she must tell herself that the dark streets are safe and that the menacing pusher is just trying to teach her a lesson. Similarly, the victim of domestic violence could not go home at night if she saw her husband for the abuser he was, nor could the child fall asleep at night if she accurately perceived her older brother as a drunken rapist. Self-protective lying allows the trauma survivor to make it through another day. An important part of recovery is learning to understand circumstances and people accurately and then applying language to describe situations, other people, and, of course, their own self. For most women in recovery from either trauma or addictions, such learning occurs in a group context where others in recovery can first apply the labels that have seemed too threatening to say out loud.

Appreciating Mutuality and Reciprocity. The final stage of interpersonal recovery begins for many women when they realize that relationships do not need to be one-sided and manipulative. Often women have experienced only relationships that are abusive and controlling, so the first step in changing a relationship pattern is to define the elements that constitute a mutual relationship. When women recognize the components of mutuality, they then need to develop strategies for developing mutual relationships, beginning with an assessment of who might be a good candidate for reciprocity and then focusing on what they will need to change in order to have a relationship characterized by genuine give-and-take.

Including Ancillary Services. A holistic, trauma-informed approach to recovery from chemical dependency necessitates that women have access to a range of ancillary services that will support their sense of empowerment and personal growth. Trauma and addiction rob women not only of a positive sense of self-worth, but also of the opportunity to traverse usual developmental milestones successfully. Many have struggled with schooling and employment and have been unable to perform the tasks required for independent living and competent parenting. When skill development opportunities are made available in these crucial areas, women can feel that they have regained some of the competencies lost as a result of trauma and addiction.

Vocational and Educational Services. As a result of addictions and long-term trauma symptoms such as dissociation, many women fail to navigate work and school placements. A trauma survivor who dissociated during class may have been labeled as having attention deficit disorder and placed in special education classes. A woman who was anxious and hypervigilant at work may have failed to complete work assignments on time and been fired.

Women in recovery may need a full range of vocational services, from job support to vocational assessment and help with interviewing and resumé writing. Moreover, women need help in dealing with work-related triggers to use substances and trauma-related triggers in the work environment. For many women, managing the interpersonal demands of a job is the most difficult aspect of working. They need assistance in reading interpersonal cues on the job and fending off unwanted advances by coworkers.

Without meaningful activity, whether full-time employment or some other alternative, women may find it difficult to sustain their new-found self-esteem. Service providers need to provide practical job-related training, but they also need to help women become aware of the link between job performance and trauma symptoms. Women need a way to understand past difficulties that does not leave them feeling incompetent or unskilled and that begins to suggest strategies for managing one's responses in a work environment.

Parenting Skills. Finkelstein, Kennedy, Thomas, and Kearns (1997) note that the desire to have and raise a healthy child is often a powerful source of motivation for women in substance abuse recovery. Yet women may be ashamed to admit that they lack the skills and the resources necessary to parent their children well. Women benefit from having access to health and educational services for their children and ample time to be with their children while they are participating in recovery programs. In residential programs, this may mean providing time for mothers and children to visit and be with one another in a range of settings. In outpatient programs, staff may need to provide child care while mothers participate in recovery programs.

Many women also benefit from pragmatic skills training on parenting. If a woman was not parented consistently and well herself, she may be at a loss for how to perform routine tasks such as feeding and changing an infant and disciplining and mentoring an adolescent. Beyond practical parenting skills, women who are trauma survivors need to consider how their trauma histories now affect their ability to parent their children. Issues with children such as limit setting, safety, and mutuality are especially difficult for women who have experienced sexual and physical abuse. Some women may find that they repeat the mistakes of their childhood with their own children, while others may discover that they make new mistakes in trying to do things differently. By understanding the impact of her own trauma history on her parenting, a woman can find creative ways of working with her child that do not raise the issues of the past. She can also learn when she needs help and give herself permission to get that help for both herself and her child.

Life Skills. Women may be ashamed to admit that because of their addictions and their trauma symptoms, they were unable to learn some of the basic life management skills necessary for independent living. Programs should provide basic training in cooking, shopping, cleaning, and money management for any woman who feels she needs help in these areas. The training should not be required for all women, since many have these skills. Peer trainers who have already been through the program can facilitate such training.

The goal in providing vocational, parenting, and life skills training goes beyond teaching particular skills and extends to repairing a woman's damaged sense of who she is. Both addiction and sexual and physical abuse leave a woman feeling bad about who she is as a woman and as a person. Ultimately this self-perception must be altered if a woman is to sustain her recovery.

Safe Housing. In addition to the services listed above, women need access to safe housing, legal services, and health care. These services may be part of a trauma-informed program, but in most cases they exist outside the program, so women will need to have assistance in gaining access to resources.

For many women, safe housing for them and their children is a top priority. Women need housing that allows them to live away from abusing domestic partners and family members and away from neighborhoods in which they used drugs and were part of a drug network. Recovery becomes all the more difficult when a woman must return to an apartment she shared with her drug-abusing boyfriend. Because of the dearth of low-income housing, women may want to consider house sharing with another woman in recovery.

Legal Services. Women may have a need for legal assistance for a variety of reasons. Some require help in obtaining restraining orders to keep abusive partners away. Others may need help with foster care or child protective services in order to regain custody of children or to terminate parental rights. Some may be dealing with charges as a result of drug-related offenses, and still others will want to take action against abusers from their past. Access to legal services gives women a sense of empowerment and control over the events in their lives.

Health Care. Health care may be the most overlooked aspect of self-care for trauma survivors and chemically addicted women. Trauma survivors are often frightened to obtain routine preventive dental and medical care because they fear making their bodies vulnerable to a health care provider. Gynecological exams, in particular, may trigger memories of an episode of sexual abuse. Substance-abusing women do great damage to their bodies in the process of satisfying their cravings, but they also suffer from poor health because many of them feel ashamed of their addiction and undeserving of good medical care.

Any program of health care in a trauma-informed addictions program should include screening for and education about human immunodeficiency virus infection. Both trauma survivors and chemically addicted women engage in behaviors that put them at risk for infection. Women need education about safer-sex practices and a chance to discuss their rights to protection in a sexual relationship. Trauma survivors who experienced violence and violation in past sexual encounters may have difficulty even contemplating the idea of a sexual relationship that is safe.

By providing access to a range of supportive services, trauma-informed addictions programs increase the chance that women will learn the skills they need in order to sustain a genuine recovery.

Avoiding Contraindicated Approaches. A trauma-informed system is defined not only by those practices that it includes but also by those that it avoids. And in an addictions program, several approaches run counter to the principles of a trauma-informed system.

Techniques that encourage an already demoralized woman to feel ashamed of herself are counterproductive, as are strategies that urge a woman to take a moral inventory and assume responsibility that may not be hers. Similarly, approaches that stress confrontation and the surrender to a higher power may make it difficult for a woman to access her own power and authority. Finally, programs that rely on intrusive monitoring to ensure compliance may violate a woman's personal space in ways that feel abusive.

By avoiding contraindicated strategies, programs create environments for women that are safe and that allow for healing and growth.

Shaming Techniques. Some recovery programs believe that it is acceptable to confront a woman with her addictive behavior by making her feel ashamed of her actions. Such programs engage in name calling and may ask women to stand in the corner, wear a dunce cap, or hang a sign around their necks declaring, "I am stupid." For trauma survivors who already feel bad about their behavior and about their essential selves, such manipulations only serve to confirm feelings of worthlessness and low self-esteem.

Moral Inventories. Recovery demands that women accept responsibility for their own behaviors and for the hurt they may have caused others. Unfortunately, many trauma survivors are all too willing to assume responsibility for actions committed by others. The young girl often feels that the abuse was her fault—that she asked for it or deserved it in some way. In a trauma-informed program, women are encouraged to do a moral inventory that includes ascribing legitimate blame to others, as well as assuming personal responsibility. Kasl (1993), in her revision of the twelve-step model for women in recovery, stresses sharing responsibility, identifying those who have done harm, and ceasing to assume responsibility for the mistakes of others.

Confrontation. For many women who have been sexually and physically abused, emotional abuse was part of the violent pattern. Perpetrators criticized, screamed, and badgered in an attempt not only to intimidate but also to break the spirit of the victim. For some women, programs that are excessively confrontational may be reminiscent of the emotional abuse they suffered at the hands of the perpetrator. Rather than being helpful, techniques that involve putting a woman on the "hot seat" may serve only to trigger a reenactment of the abuse. Confrontation should be replaced by clear and honest feedback about a woman's behavior and the impact of her actions. Such feedback should always be delivered in a manner that respects the consumer's essential dignity.

A Higher Power. Recovery programs often stress that the consumer turn over control to a power more forceful than either she or the drug she is abusing. Certainly an honest recognition of what can and cannot be controlled is an important part of healing, but an acceptance of a higher power cannot come at the expense of personal power. For many trauma survivors, the task is not to give up power but to assume legitimate power and control. Kasl (1993) suggests that a higher power be viewed as awakening personal power and that women be given the tools and the authority to take charge of their lives and stop submitting to the will of others.

Intrusive Monitoring. In some residential addictions programs, especially those administered by the criminal justice system, monitoring is a routine part of guaranteeing compliance. Women may be asked to provide urine samples under the supervision of male staff, or they may have to strip for an inspection and have their body cavities searched for contraband. All activities that violate personal boundaries and are experienced as abusive and retraumatizing should be avoided in a trauma-informed program. Staff members need to balance their need to know if a woman is using drugs with the woman's need to have her body respected. Less intrusive monitoring, which may involve behavioral observations, should be substituted, and if urine samples need to be monitored, a same-sex staff person should do the monitoring.

Conclusion

Creating trauma-informed addictions programming may require many aspects of a program to be modified or changed entirely. Yet without these changes we rely on programs and methodologies that run the risk of retraumatizing women and perpetuating a life of abuse and addiction.

References

Amaro, H., Freed, L., Cabral, H., and Zuckerman, B. "Violence During Pregnancy and Substance Use." *American Journal of Public Health,* 1990, *80*(5), 575–579.

Coleman, E. "Child Physical and Sexual Abuse Among Chemically Dependent Individuals." In E. Coleman (ed.), *Chemical Dependency and Intimacy Dysfunction.* New York: Haworth Press, 1987.

Drabble, L. "Elements of Effective Services for Women." In B. Underhill and D. Finnegan (eds.), *Chemical Dependency: Women at Risk.* New York: Harrington Park Press, 1996.

Evans, K., and Sullivan, J. M. *Treating Addicted Survivors of Trauma.* New York: Guilford Press, 1995.

Finkelstein, N. "Using the Relational Model as a Context for Treating Pregnant Parenting and Chemically Dependent Women." In B. Underhill and D. Finnegan (eds.), *Chemical Dependency: Women at Risk.* New York: Harrington Park Press, 1996.

Finkelstein, N., Kennedy, C., Thomas, K., and Kearns, M. *Gender-Specific Substance Abuse Treatment.* Alexandria, Va.: National Women's Resource Center for Prevention and Treatment of Alcohol, Tobacco, and Other Drug Abuse and Mental Illness, 1997.

Goodman, L., Dutton, M., and Harris, M. "Physical and Sexual Assault Prevalence Among Episodically Homeless Women with Serious Mental Illness." *American Journal of Orthopsychiatry,* 1995, *65*(4), 468–478.

Herman, J. *Trauma and Recovery.* New York: Basic Books, 1992.

Jordan, J., and others (eds.) *Women's Growth in Connection.* New York: Guilford Press, 1991.

Kasl, C. D. *Many Roads, One Journey: Moving Beyond the Twelve Steps.* New York: HarperCollins, 1993.

Office of Justice Programs, Bureau of Justice Statistics. *Violence Against Women: A National Crime Victimization Survey Report.* Washington, D.C.: U.S. Department of Justice, 1994.

Root, M. P. P. "Treatment Failures: Root of Sexual Victimization in Women's Addictive Behavior." *American Journal of Orthopsychiatry,* 1989, *59,* 542–549.

Wallen, J., and Berman, K. "Possible Indicators of Childhood Sexual Abuse for Individuals in Substance Abuse Treatment." *Journal of Child Sexual Abuse,* 1992, *1*(3), 63–74.

MAXINE HARRIS *is codirector of Community Connections in Washington, D.C., and executive director of its National Capital Center for Trauma Recovery and Empowerment.*

ROGER D. FALLOT *is codirector of Community Connections.*

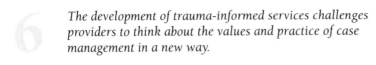

The development of trauma-informed services challenges providers to think about the values and practice of case management in a new way.

Trauma-Informed Services and Case Management

David W. Freeman

The very label *case management* becomes an outmoded concept in a trauma-informed service delivery system. The language of "case" (as opposed to human being) and "management" (as opposed to help, education, facilitation, support, and encouragement) can be insensitive to many issues that are important to trauma-informed services.

To be trauma informed is to be aware of power, control, and interpersonal boundary issues in the clinical relationship. Although it is true that actual abuse happens in professional relationships, the subtler and more implicit abuses are the primary focus of this chapter. Trauma-informed service providers seek to be aware of the dynamics of abuse and to prevent those dynamics from being recreated in an otherwise helpful relationship.

Four clusters of values can differentiate traditional case management from trauma-informed services in an effective way: power and control, authority, goals, and language.

Power and Control

Trauma frequently entails experiences of powerlessness and loss of control. Consumer-survivors often bring specific sensitivities to the ways in which power and control dynamics are expressed in clinical relationships.

Management versus Empowerment. Power and control are vested in the staff in traditional case management. Case managers typically author the treatment plan, which governs access to clinical resources and requires the consumer's attendance at treatment appointments. Housing directors establish detailed residential rules that control, direct, and limit everyday behavior. The representative payee controls the expenditure of even the smallest amounts of money. Psychiatric appointments are often scheduled with case manager and consumer together to improve communication, but at the expense of the consumer's privacy and her control over her own personal story.

Case management offers a risk-free life to people who accept its services. The representative payee pays rent and utilities, one's personal history is told by another to the psychiatrist, and compliance with house rules ensures trouble-free housing. Such risk-reducing management activities will be soothing to some. However, these management functions can be extremely burdensome to abuse survivors, recreating the controlling relationship that they first experienced at the hands of a perpetrator many years before. "Well-managed" case management services can also close off opportunities for learning through life's natural consequences. Some abuse survivors and professionals who have a history of avoiding risks are glad for the opportunity to take a chance in the supportive environment of a trauma-informed system.

In trauma-informed service systems, power and control are vested in the consumer. Thus, the process of consumer empowerment requires clinicians to yield some of their power to the consumer. Collaboration and cooperation are central concepts here. Service plans, housing arrangements, financial decisions, and medication orders are negotiated between professional and consumer. The consumer's voice, which has often been silenced, is nurtured and amplified so that it can be clearly heard. Clinicians find a new respect for consumers as the process of empowerment unfolds, and this respect facilitates a richer empowerment of the consumer.

Julie's story: At first I was worried about working in a trauma-informed system. I found myself taking personal and professional risks that I had never seriously entertained in the past. For example, I found that I could not hide behind a professional mask. I had to share much more of myself and become a real person in the eyes of the consumers around me. The empowerment of others requires me to yield some of my own power and control.

Problems and Disabilities versus Strengths. Traditional case management focuses on the problems and disabilities of consumers. Most treatment plans in this model start with a problem list that clarifies the nature and scope of treatment. This deficit orientation, which emphasizes the aspects of a person that are broken and dysfunctional, diminishes the power and authority of the individual who is being served and reinforces the need for an expert clinician to set things right.

The problem list approach to treatment planning and intervention generally blames the consumer. This blaming posture again reinforces the dynamics that many survivors of abuse first experienced in childhood. The notions of blame, problem, and incapacity also reassert the unequal power relationship between professional and consumer.

The trauma-informed system values a strengths-based approach to assessment and intervention that highlights the assets of the consumer.

Instead of being defined by his or her problems, the consumer is described as having capacities and abilities. All human beings have strengths, but strengths can be invisible or even undermined if they are not acknowledged and supported. A strengths-based perspective effectively facilitates the development of more skill and capacity in the individual, promoting a sense of well-being, competence, and self-esteem. The experience of a sense of competence sets in motion a further change process, helping consumers to appreciate their own abilities. It can be enormously beneficial to an individual to develop an inventory of her positive qualities, and a strengths-based perspective helps set this in motion.

John's story: When I facilitated my first trauma group, I was amazed at the intensity and power of the survivors in the group. I had previously thought that survivors were disabled and inarticulate. My main experience of people had been in the traditional medical model setting, where their voices could not be clearly heard. I will never again make the mistake of underestimating the strength of survivors.

Symptom Management and Reduction versus Skills Building. The traditional case management treatment plan calls for the reduction of problematic symptoms by a certain percentage. Such a plan will state that aggressive behavior, for example, or hallucinated voices will decrease by 10 percent in the next six months. The symptom is generally isolated from the consumer's life context and is rarely appreciated for the functions it serves.

This strategy of symptom management compartmentalizes and objectifies behavior and takes it out of its meaningful context. When the sense of a behavior's intention and purpose is lost, the person is devalued. The belief that one has behaved in a way that makes sense under adverse, abusive circumstances is also lost.

A trauma-informed approach emphasizes the skills that consumers could usefully acquire. The focus is on the future and the capacity for the development of new resources. A skills-building approach cultivates an environment of hopefulness, which contributes to the overall potential for recovery.

Authority and Responsibility

Trauma survivors are often especially attuned to possible abuses of authority and to practices that assign responsibility or blame inappropriately.

Expert Intervention versus Psychoeducation. In traditional case management, interventions are designed by experts with training in social work, psychology, psychiatry, or administration. They may give advice, direction, and orders to consumers, who are sometimes seen as being unaware of what is best for them. Explanations of behavior may be based in biological, psychodynamic, behavioral, or family systems models. In each case, the consumer cannot hope to know as much as the professional, who has devoted years to learning a clinical language and rationale.

Abusive relationships depend on unequal distribution of power in the relationship. The clinician as expert may unwittingly recreate the dynamics of the abusive relationship as expertise facilitates the exercise of power over another. When authority resides primarily in the clinician in the helping relationship, it becomes difficult for the consumer to trust herself enough to develop a voice of her own.

The sharing of information in a psychoeducational program that is both interactive and flexible enough to accommodate what the consumer thinks is important in a trauma-informed system. A psychoeducational program introduces consumers to the explanatory power of a trauma-informed clinical conceptualization. In such an educational program, past abuses are linked to current coping strategies, and current symptoms are reframed as attempts to cope with past abuses. Psychoeducational programs are most effective in group settings where consumers can learn from each other as well as staff, and staff can learn from the consumer's perspective. A group-based psychoeducational program also helps consumers trust their own perceptions of reality and receive validation for correct perceptions.

Allocation of Resources Driven by the System versus the Consumer. In a traditional case management program, the allocation of resources is often determined by a central clinical authority that is charged with the responsibility of keeping the gates and controlling who receives which service. These authorities often develop labyrinthine application procedures that require the practical assistance and advocacy of expert case managers. The average consumer can easily be made dependent on the system even for help in deciphering and interpreting the system's rules.

In a trauma-informed system, the allocation of resources is driven by consumer request. This demands a degree of flexibility in intervention planning that may be difficult to achieve in traditional systems. Consumers are empowered to direct their own lives in trauma-informed systems. At every opportunity, the consumer is brought into the decision-making process. Clinical services, housing arrangements, financial management strategies, and psychiatric services are all coordinated around the expressed needs of the consumer.

Goals

A trauma-informed approach encourages clinicians to rethink many traditional service goals.

Stabilization versus Growth and Change. Traditional case management values stabilization. Explosive behavior, the expression of intense affect, and withdrawal from interpersonal relationships are all understood as symptoms that require intervention. The clinician's goal in traditional case management is to ameliorate these symptoms, smoothing the path for the consumer's restabilization or return to the mainstream.

Survivors of abuse have legitimate protests about the use and abuse of power and control by professional systems. Yet professionals might interpret these protests as symptoms of a mental illness that require stabilization. In trauma-informed services, professionals can see these protests as an energetic and legitimate rejection of the status quo. Trauma-informed services value growth and change. The expression of powerful affect is understood as a reasonable effort to cope with difficult experiences. It is understood that intense feeling and self-expression have successfully protected the individual from past abuses. The goal now is to capitalize on the individual's underlying desire for a safer environment and a better life. Trauma-informed service providers help consumers develop their advocacy skills so that they can more effectively get what they want and help other trauma survivors as well.

Language

In trauma-informed systems, clinicians use language that communicates the values of consumer-survivor empowerment and recovery.

Clinical Language versus Everyday Language. Language provides support to those who are in power. "Doctors" and "professionals" are immediately thought of as having more power, knowledge, and authority than "patients." When "patients" are described as "chronically mentally ill (CMI)," there is an underlying suggestion that they are weak and deficient.

Wherever possible, trauma-informed providers talk about people and consumers rather than "patients" or "CMI adults." Daily language changes so that *plan of action* replaces *treatment plan, personal history* replaces *assessment,* and *narrative of events* replaces *progress notes* or *contact logs.* Changes in everyday language help clinicians become more aware of the stigma and power maintained by traditional discourse.

Chris's story: Change in the use of language takes time. I sometimes forget to use the new language, especially when I get nervous or upset. When I fall back on the traditional language, I often feel humiliated. I notice the impact of language all the time now. There is a consciousness raising that happens. I think people rally around a new way of describing and thinking about themselves. At the same time, I can see them wilt when they are described in the same old words.

Trauma-Informed Service Systems: Practical Applications

A greater awareness of trauma-related concerns can lead to particular modifications in a number of common clinical interventions.

Treatment Planning versus Service Contracts. Traditional treatment plans invoke the authority of scientific practice by articulating a diagnosis and problem list. This plan, however, may obscure the fact that there was and is a process of negotiation and uncertainty that accompanies clinical work and decision making.

Elaine's story: I always hated signing my treatment plan. The forms were long and confusing, and I usually ended up signing them without reading them.

The parts of the form that I did understand were insulting. I don't like talking about my problems with people I don't really know. Sometimes I had to sign the form after a long meeting with a lot of people: my psychiatrist, a social worker, some nurses—and the psych tech who put me in the quiet area last week! I never felt that I had much of a choice. And I knew that if I refused to sign, I would never get a job or an apartment—and those were the things I really wanted. They have to do these forms, I guess. Otherwise they couldn't get paid. But the forms don't do me any good.

The challenge for the trauma-informed service provider is to create a contract that helps bring the consumer's voice to life. This can be accomplished in several ways. The contract can be transparent about the process that helped produce the document. In trauma-informed work, this process involves negotiation of goals and strategic actions. If this process can be articulated, the voices of the consumer and the clinician, and the relationship between them, is brought out into the open. The contract can help empower consumers by focusing on consumer strengths, resources, and hopes rather than diagnoses and disabilities.

A pilot project at Community Connections has developed the Consumer Action and Support Plan (CASPAR) as an alternative to the traditional treatment plan. The CASPAR abandons problem lists as a starting point and focuses instead on consumer goals, the strengths and resources that the consumer brings to the table for achieving those goals, and the supports needed from staff to facilitate progress toward those goals. Additional skills that might enable the consumer to achieve these goals more easily are then described.

The second section of the CASPAR details the clinician's goals, the consumer's reaction to those goals, and the negotiated settlement. The agendas of the different parties—and their power relations—are always clearly stated in the CASPAR. The processes by which differences of opinion are resolved are made clear.

Darlene's story: I like it when people ask me what I want, particularly if I am taken seriously when I speak out. My old treatment team hated me. I argued with them all the time, and sometimes I got violent and threw things at them. The main problem was that we always disagreed, and I never got what I wanted. The old team reminded me of my family. They acted as if they knew what was best for me, but never asked how I felt or what I wanted. Believe me, I will fight tooth and nail against people who remind me of them. I care about being respected, and I demand to be taken seriously.

Crisis Planning and Response. Crisis intervention in traditional case management programs is focused on controlling the consumer and protecting the community. Sometimes force is used. Psychiatrists, psychologists, the courts, and the police can arrange for forced, involuntary hospitalization. Hospitals can keep people against their will. The potential for forceful imposition of authority and control (through commitment, restraint, and seclusion) is either active or threatened. The imposition of violent restraint techniques may even result in injury to the consumer.

A core feature of trauma is the experience of being overpowered by others. The ability to defend interpersonal boundaries is regularly threatened and breached in a traumatic relationship. Trauma survivors often report that the crisis intervention strategies of traditional case management programs are retraumatizing.

Barbara's story: I don't remember everything that happened before I was last hospitalized, but I do know I had a lot of problems. I was experimenting with a lower dose of medication because I didn't like the side effects, my boyfriend was beating me up, and my roommate had stolen my money. My case manager showed up with the police to take me to the hospital. I hate the hospital, and I hate the police. Basically I like to be in charge of myself.

In trauma-informed service systems, the consumer is invited to participate in crisis planning. Soothing activities are identified in advance, as are consumer choices about the specific interventions used to defuse a crisis. Skills in avoiding and deescalating crisis situations are identified and learned. Consumers are helped to take the opportunity to think into the future, plan for bad times, manage and protect their own boundaries, and take responsibility for making choices. All of these activities are empowering for the consumer.

Money Management. Money is often regarded as a necessary evil in traditional case management. There is almost never enough of it, and what little there is can easily become a battleground between case manager and consumer. It is not unusual for consumers to have only seventy dollars per month of discretionary money (after rent, utilities, food, and telephone) and for that money to be tightly controlled in small increments. This level of control is often introduced as a well-meaning attempt to protect the consumer against running out of money before the end of the month. In traditional case management, entitlement money is sometimes used as a reward for approved behaviors.

Money management occupies an intimate space in our lives. Many of our needs are met through the acquisition and expenditure of money. For another to have authority over this personal space can easily lead to boundary violations. Many trauma survivors have difficult experiences with people who assume positions of authority and then function in an over- or undercontrolling fashion. Peremptory, abrupt, or severe authority can be reminiscent of trauma experiences. Consumers who are hostile to the imposition of financial controls are sometimes criticized for their impulsivity, their anger management problems, or their noncompliance. In fact, they may simply be asserting authority over a medium of exchange with others.

Paula's story: Nothing is more important to me than my money. I don't trust anyone else to manage my money for me. I have friends who got ripped off by other agencies. One agency stole thousands of dollars from consumers. I know I don't always make the right decisions, but I would rather live with my own mistakes than have somebody else tell me what I can and can't have. My case manager used to give me ten dollars if I came to my appointment. To tell you the

*truth, it was exactly like my old boyfriend. If I did what my boyfriend wanted,
I'd get paid. And otherwise I'd get beaten up. Lots of times my boyfriend paid me
for sex. I don't like anything that reminds me of those days.*

In a trauma-informed system, the clinician uses the management of
money as a tool to facilitate empowerment. Opportunities to use money
management training to support the development of skills in dealing with
interpersonal boundaries and responsibilities are legion.

As consumers assume increasing responsibility, clinicians begin to take
greater risks. It is important that the clinician be actively involved in
explaining the risks of financial decisions and increasing supports if consumers make bad decisions. As consumers learn more about the choice
points in money management, they are empowered to shape their own lives
more effectively.

Conclusion

Trauma-informed clinicians work in an environment that is traditional in
its values and principles and must therefore be responsive to the concerns
of the traditional mental health authorities. In fact, they must be able to
operate in two worlds at the same time: the integrity of trauma services
must be maintained, and the needs of the traditional system must be
addressed. In addition, they must translate back and forth between the two
worlds, explaining, for example, the importance of empowerment and
strengths on the one hand, while helping the consumer maintain needed
benefits on the other.

In order for clinicians to become trauma informed, they must immerse
themselves in a new way of thinking about service delivery. Clinical for-
mulations, relationships with consumers, the language of treatment planning, money management, and crisis intervention strategies—to name just
a few domains—are different. The challenge of maintaining competence in
the traditional system while developing skills in trauma-informed services
is intellectually and emotionally challenging.

It is important for clinicians to work together with other professionals
and with consumers to cultivate a support system that is adequate to meet
these challenges. As clinicians bring trauma-informed values into the workplace, the rewards become obvious. The rejection of the old paradigm can
be exciting. The cultivation of a new sense of purpose and mission is invig-
orating. And perhaps most important, consumers are gratified and inspired
by the change in culture and the introduction of a new and compelling set
of values and practices.

DAVID W. FREEMAN *is director of Creative Connections, a program of Community Connections in Washington, D.C.*

*This chapter provides pragmatic recommendations for
creating partnerships with recipients of services who have
traditionally been the most silent stakeholders in mental
health system design and service delivery.*

Defining the Role
of Consumer-Survivors
in Trauma-Informed Systems

Laura Prescott

Establishing the right to equal representation and participation, freedom
from discrimination, and self-determination contributed heavily to the
language of the consumer/survivor/ex-patient movement in the 1970s
and Americans With Disabilities Act of 1990. Recent support for recovery and trauma-sensitive approaches emphasizing the principles of empowerment and self-determination in mental health coalesce with a
number of other important social and economic shifts affecting the efforts
of human service agencies to integrate consumer-survivors.

Managed care, privatization, blended funding streams, and emphasis on research-based outcomes have provided new opportunities for
consumer-survivor involvement. Related emphasis on developing performance improvement measures and ensuring accountability can dramatically increase consumer-survivor involvement at all levels of policy
and practice. Although many clinicians, administrators, and policymakers have embraced the principles of integration, they have struggled with
defining what that means and how to proceed. Within this context,
many human service agencies are challenged to stretch their vision
beyond deficit-based approaches, search for new ways to operationalize
the values of empowerment, and co-create cultures that foster sustainable partnerships with those receiving services.

Much of the material contained in this chapter is derived from L. Prescott, *Consumer/
Survivor/Recovering Women: A Guide for New Partners in Collaboration.* Delmar, N.Y.:
Women, Co-Occurring Disorders and Violence Coordinating Center, forthcoming.

Benefits of Involving Consumer-Survivors

The benefits of integrating consumer-survivors into all levels of system and service and evaluation efforts range from improving the quality of services and performance improvement to increasing overall organizational efficacy (McCabe and Unzicker, 1995; Campbell, 1993; Fisher, 1994; Deegan, 1995). Operationalizing empowerment within agencies by promoting inclusion strengthens research design, training methods, policy sensitivity, and collaboration among multiple stakeholders (Van Tosh and others, 1993; McCabe and Unzicker, 1995; Prescott, forthcoming). In addition, consumer-survivors cite individual benefits as well, including opportunities to redefine their relationship to authority, decrease isolation, and increase self-esteem.

Barriers to Involvement

In order to generate innovative strategies to involvement, consumer-survivors and other key stakeholders have explored some of the barriers. The discussion that follows seeks to spark increased cross-constituency dialogue and provide a preliminary framework for facilitating similar integration efforts in the future.

Access. Agency personnel and recipients define problems of access in very different ways. Multistakeholders often indicate they are not aware of available consumer-survivors, although many provided services to hundreds of women with substance abuse, mental health, and trauma histories. Internalization of professional training that emphasizes deficit-based orientation and diagnostics can be a barrier to perceiving recipients as partners, allies, and experts.

Consumer-survivors relate problems of access to all other barriers mentioned here. Access is defined in terms of financial remuneration for child care, transportation, food costs, and time spent associated with projects (Rapp, Shera, and Kisthardt, 1993; McCabe and Unzicker, 1995; Van Tosh and others, 1993; Prescott, forthcoming). Poverty and isolation frequently prohibit access to communication technology and pertinent program information, perpetuating a lack of familiarity with agency goals and personnel and contributing to the high rates of attrition among consumer-survivors.

Disclosure, Safety, and Stigma. Discussions regarding disclosure raise strong emotions. Until recently, few individuals in professional and nonprofessional positions with psychiatric diagnoses have felt free to disclose their mental health histories. Fisher (1994) articulates both the efficacy of disclosure to influence policy and the frequent negative impact of revealing psychiatric diagnoses and experiences of institutionalization. Many consumer-survivors express a strong desire to share their firsthand experiences, particularly when the information meaningfully contributes to improving system designs and service delivery for others. However, stigma and the related tendency to pathologize individuals who reveal their mental health conditions discourage dialogue and reinforce silence. Because disclosure is linked with perceptions of safety, which in turn are associated with feeling validated, believed, and acknowledged (Fisher, 1994), it can be a useful measure of environmental tolerance and support for increasing diversity. In this era that emphasizes measurable outcomes and accountability, self-determination, and concepts of recovery, the discourse pertaining to disclosure and safety will necessarily intensify.

Language, Tokenism, and Information. Childhood abuse and adult revictimization assault spiritual, physical, and emotional integrity in ways that can devastate self-esteem, trust, and hope. Perhaps one of the most insidious long-term effects is the internalized message of devaluation. Writings by consumer-survivors and others underscore the ways in which these messages are often reinforced through psychiatric labeling, routine, and crisis intervention. Because of these experiences, consumer-survivors often possess a heightened awareness and sensitivity to expressed and covert environmental devaluation.

Decreasing isolation, supporting positive role modeling, promoting public partnerships, influencing policy and practice, and strengthening system and research accountability are all enriched in environments where consumer-survivors feel safe enough to contribute their expertise meaningfully. Language and the implicit messages of conveyed power significantly affect the extent of articulated safety that consumer-survivors note. The use of diagnostic terminology such as "the" CMI (chronically mentally ill), SMI (seriously mentally ill), or SPMI (seriously and persistently mentally ill) is consistently associated with experiences of "spirit-breaking" (Deegan, 1990).

Competence, Relevance, Fear of Anger, and Boundaries. There is an intimate connection among unspoken concerns regarding consumer-survivor capabilities to become active partners, fear of anger, and confusion about the relevance of integration efforts and boundaries. Professional training is often imbued with deficit orientation, negative media stereotypes, and distance from direct professional interaction with consumer-survivors. This training makes it difficult to see the capacities, strengths, and contributions of consumer-survivors. Tensions mount when misunderstood behaviors and feelings (such as anger) are mistakenly assigned to personal pathology rather than assessing contextual factors. As with any other new relationship, developing partnerships takes time and skill in boundary negotiation. Both consumer-survivors and mental health providers are challenged to find new ways to relate to one another based on changing power dynamics.

Recommended Strategies for Creating New Partnerships

Many agencies may value diversity and understand the benefits of integrating consumer-survivors, but they are unsure about how to operationalize those values in concrete steps that lead to sustainable involvement over time.

Plan Proactively. Proactive planning can greatly decrease the unanticipated chaos that ensues with organizational shifts. Meeting with multiple stakeholders early and encouraging open dialogue about their concerns creates buy-in and facilitates identification of potential barriers to successful consumer-survivor integration. Strong leadership, clear administrative messages about the efficacy of integration, and opportunities for open dialogue about potential conflict areas are important preliminary steps in preparing the organizational culture for change. Assessing the relative strengths and needs in the environment and adapting values clarification instruments to identify areas of conflict and commonality among members also facilitate future discussions regarding integration.

Create a Strategic Plan. Creating a template for consumer-survivor involvement with an agency team facilitates discussions and contributes to structural buy-in. Strategic plans help operationalize the agency mission and vision in concrete terms that are measurable.

Define Terms. Defining *involvement, integration, consumer-survivor, significant,* and *representation* is important in generating standards to guide implementation over time. Definitions highlight priorities and make essential distinctions between former recipients of services and "secondary consumer groups" such as family members and other advocates. These individuals frequently "speak for" consumer-survivors, often without their endorsement.

Baseline and gold standards for involvement establish parameters within which change and ongoing quality assurance can be internally reviewed. Some demonstration projects have used 50 percent of consumer-survivor participation as a target for involvement, while others have recommended at least 33 percent (McCabe and Unzicker, 1995).

Measure and Monitor Progress. One of the benefits of building a strategic plan that measures and monitors progress is the ability to show improved outcomes, which can lead to opportunities for future funding. Forums concentrating on measuring and monitoring consumer-survivor integration activities and the generation of consumer-survivor self-report scales are two strategies used to integrate involvement efforts with ongoing quality assurance processes.

Work Toward Sustainability. Increasing the number of role models and mentors decreases isolation and burn-out and increases diversity and retention. Increasing the presence of consumer-survivors in various roles generates energy, fosters sustainability, encourages interest, and provides opportunities for in-house staff to confront common stereotypes of homogeneity and incompetence associated with those who have been psychiatrically diagnosed.

Review Policies. A review of policies can lead to policy adaptations that obviate potential misunderstanding and organizational resentment. Policies of particular interest are those that focus on benefits, contracting, budget and hiring.

Adapt Medical and Bereavement Benefits. Revisiting the structure of medical and leave-of-absence benefits reflects sensitivity to the fluctuating needs and extreme conditions in the lives of consumer-survivors. Unanticipated leave may become necessary in substance use relapse, medication adjustment, reengagement in psychiatric treatment, periods of physical decline associated with human immunodeficiency virus, and becoming a victim of violence.

Death, rejection, and distance have often required consumer-survivors to redefine family in unconventional terms. Supportive networks, extended family, and close friends regularly constitute primary intimate support in the lives of former recipients of services. Policies governing bereavement leave tend to extend benefits from solely the immediate family to include many consumer-survivor-defined family members.

Extend Hiring Policies. Creating a substitution clause in hiring policies allowing lived experience and other relevant expertise to replace academic degrees broadens the scope of candidates for consideration. Similarly, flexible work provisions are recommended to enhance work production, cost savings, and individual satisfaction.

Allocate Money for Consumer-Survivor Development. Some of the expenses associated with the early stages of involving consumer-survivors are recruitment, training, travel, and interpreters for those who have physical disabilities or for whom English is not a first language.

Hire and Compensate at Competitive Wages. The lack of formal consumer-survivor positions either within agency structures or by contract makes it less likely that recipient involvement will be sustainable over time. Involving consumer-survivors as advisers in board meetings, focus groups, and other voluntary activities is important to program endeavors. However, advisers generally volunteer their time and do not make decisions; moreover, their presence does not fundamentally change the shape of structural power imbalances. In order for consumer-survivors to become partners in mental health service delivery, they need to be active members in policy, planning, funding, and research arenas where decisions are made. Many former recipients of services have busy lives and multiple responsibilities that restrict their ability to devote unlimited amounts of time and energy to program tasks. Hiring consumer-survivors at competitive salaries with adequate benefits alleviates tension arising from competition for time.

Create a Range of Roles with Clearly Defined Responsibilities. A wide range of innovative and socially valued positions and associated tasks has evolved in local and national projects attempting to integrate consumer-survivors into the fabric of service design and delivery. Broad categories include executive management, training and education, research and evaluation, community education and development, service delivery and outreach, knowledge development, monitoring and oversight, and volunteer activities.

Many consumer-survivors have traumatic histories of being exposed to erratic environments and conflicting performance expectations. Therefore, clearly defined roles with articulated responsibilities, tasks, and performance measures create environmental predictability, optimizing opportunities for individual success, bolstered self-esteem, and sense of safety.

Provide Orientation and Leadership Development. Orientation, leadership, skills development, and cross-training have been used to promote buy-in, generate enthusiasm, provide ongoing information, model partnerships between consumer-survivors and agency personnel, and develop team cohesiveness. Some of the most successful delivery models have used train-the-trainer approaches and consumer-survivor cofacilitation.

Tailor the Meeting Environment. Creating accessible and welcoming environments fosters consumer-survivor participation in meetings that have not traditionally considered former recipients of services as key stakeholders.

Plan Enough Time. Becoming an active partner in any process usually requires time and attention to power dynamics affecting the relative equilibrium between participating members. Consumer-survivors, particularly women and individuals representing cultures that value group cohesiveness and conformity over individuality and personal independence, may be reticent to offer their opinions. Abusive histories coupled with experiences of social, economic, and political devaluation can leave consumer-survivors cautious, self-conscious, and afraid of reprisal. Scheduling enough time for consumer-survivors to participate and reflecting back what they say conveys important implicit and respectful messages regarding valuable contributions.

Hold Meetings in Neutral Places. Meetings scheduled in treatment centers, psychiatric facilities, or other restricted institutional settings can restimulate difficult experiences. The presence of power, authority, threat of force, and coercion will influence the extent of direct, honest dialogue needed in true partnership endeavors. Be cautious about assuming treatment settings are "safe," "convenient" places to meet with individuals still in treatment, particularly if they are in locked settings.

Adapt Physical Spaces. Although individual responses to room design vary tremendously, some common themes continually emerge. Avoid blocking entries and exits, overcrowding, and sitting behind consumer-survivor women. Because some seating arrangements may be more comfortable than others, ask former recipients how to set up the room prior to the meeting. (Prescott, forthcoming).

Document the Process. Documenting the process from the beginning provides invaluable insight into the strategies employed, barriers encountered, lessons learned, and new approaches developed to achieve the best possible outcome. Multimedia approaches (videotaping, recorded oral histories, theater, scrapbooks, and poetry readings, for example) have been highly effective in preserving a historical record, passing information on to individuals who cannot attend meetings, and advertising integration efforts.

Conclusion

There are still many questions left to be answered pertaining to creating environments that foster a sustainable presence of consumer-survivors in all phases of mental health system design and service delivery. Critical new knowledge continues to emerge at local and national levels as consumer-survivors, clinicians, policymakers, administrators, and researchers work together to operationalize their commitment to increasing partnerships and sustained involvement.

References

Campbell, J. "From Lab Rat to Researcher: The History, Models, and Policy Implications of Consumer/Survivor Involvement in Research." Proceedings of the Fourth Annual National Conference on State Mental Health Agency Services Research and Program Evaluation. Alexandria, Va.: National Association of State Mental Health Program Directors Research Institute, October 2–5, 1993.

Deegan, P. E. "Spirit Breaking: When the Helping Professional Hurt." *Humanistic Psychologist*, 1990, *18*(3), 301–313.

Deegan, P. E. "Recovery as a Journey of the Heart." Paper presented at Recovery from Psychiatric Disability: Implication for the Training of Mental Health Professionals, Boston, Mass., May 10, 1995.

Fisher, D. B. "A New Vision of Healing as Constructed by People with Psychiatric Disabilities Working as Mental Health Providers." *Psychosocial Rehabilitation Journal*, 1994, *17*(3), pp. 67–81.

McCabe, S., and Unzicker, R. E. "Changing Roles of Consumer/Survivors in Mature Mental Health Systems." In L. I. Stein and E. J. Hollingsworth (eds.) *Maturing Mental Health Systems: New Challenges and Opportunities*. New Directions for Mental Health Services, no. 66. San Francisco: Jossey-Bass, 1995.

Prescott, L. *Consumer/Survivor/Recovering Women: A Guide for New Partners in Collaboration*. Delmar, N.Y.: Women, Co-Occurring Disorders and Violence Coordinating Center, forthcoming.

Rapp, C. A., Shera, W., and Kisthardt, W. "Research Strategies for Consumer Empowerment of People with Severe Mental Illness." *Social Work*, 1993, *38*(6), 727–735.

Van Tosh, L., and others. *Working for a Change: Employment of Consumer/Survivors in the Design and Provision of Services for Persons Who Are Homeless and Mentally Disabled*. Washington, D.C.: Center for Mental Health Services, Substance Abuse and Mental Health Services Administration, July 1993.

LAURA PRESCOTT *is the former assistant director of the Women, Co-Occurring Disorders and Violence Coordinating Center and current founder of Sister Witness International. A psychiatric ex-patient and survivor of abuse, she has been in substance abuse recovery for many years.*

*Effective services for trauma survivors rely on addressing
the support and care needs of clinicians and administrators.*

Care of the Clinician

Ellen Arledge, Rebecca Wolfson

Clinician self-care is an important aspect of a trauma-informed system. In a trauma-informed system the human dimension should always be at the forefront, with consideration given to the whole person, regardless of whether that person is a consumer, a clinician, or a program administrator. The clinician, like the consumer, has strengths, needs, concerns, and vulnerabilities. Whether the clinician is a case manager, vocational counselor, or addictions counselor, the nature of working closely with trauma survivors requires that the individual pay special attention to personal boundary maintenance and self-care. High prevalence rates of abuse among the men and women served make it important for program planners and clinicians alike to look at the impact of this work on the providers. Moreover, the lack of emphasis on clinician self-care may be a contributing factor to the frequent turnover of frontline workers in traditional human service delivery systems.

In order to provide the most compassionate care for consumers, individual clinicians and their agencies need to recognize, understand, and address signs of stress in the clinician. A number of terms have been used to describe the phenomenon of clinician stress: *burnout, compassion fatigue, vicarious traumatization,* and *countertransference.* Generally those who are using these terms are speaking about the change in the clinician's internal experience that results from responsibility for and empathic engagement with traumatized consumers. The specific impact for each clinician is determined by the unique interaction between the situation and the person of the clinician (Pearlman and Saakvitne, 1995). Unfortunately, *burnout* and *compassion fatigue* have developed the negative connotation that the clinician is weak or callous, and *vicarious traumatization* has been interpreted as meaning that the consumer herself is traumatizing or toxic to the clinician.

We instead use the term *impact of trauma work* (ITW) to describe this aspect of working with trauma survivors.

The Impact of Trauma Work on Clinicians

ITW can influence clinicians in a number of ways. It can distort and change their worldview, threaten their sense of personal safety and foster paranoia, disrupt their sense of spiritual connectedness, and physically and emotionally exhaust them, thus depleting much needed inner resources.

Although we may sometimes be unaware of the hidden assumptions that make up our view of how the world works, we all have a naive philosophy that determines how we make sense of the world. We may, for example, believe that the world is a fair place and that people who work hard and behave well will be rewarded. Or we may start with an assumption that the world and the behaviors of those of us in it consist of a series of events that occur randomly, almost independent of the actions of others. Regardless of the worldview, it is almost impossible for anyone to work with the survivors of profound sexual and physical abuse and not have that worldview altered. Over time, clinicians may notice, or their friends and family may become aware, that they no longer seem to hold the same beliefs about the world. Others may remark that they seem jaded or pessimistic in outlook. They may become so cynical as to conclude that moral principles are useless. Clinicians may even become angry at consumers for challenging their worldview.

A worker's sense of personal safety can also become distorted, and she can find herself becoming paranoid about others' intentions. After a few years of working in a homeless shelter, a clinician told her supervisor, "I just can't take it anymore. It seems like every woman I know has been raped or battered. Now, when I make a new friend I wonder, When is she going to tell me she was abused? I practically assume men are going to hurt me. The world just seems like a dirtier place to me."

This loss of a sense of safety can affect one's professional behavior. A clinician may become more authoritarian and directive and lose sight of the larger therapeutic task of empowerment. Rather than developing a consumer's ability to self-protect, the clinician may assume an authoritarian role. The clinician may become fearful and overly protective, cautioning consumers that danger lurks everywhere and that they must always be vigilant. If, on the other hand, the clinician copes with feeling unsafe by numbing her own awareness of danger, she may fail to make distinctions about unsafe situations and therefore fail to help consumers sharpen skills to recognize and negotiate unsafe situations (Pearlman and Saakvitne, 1995).

Finally, the ITW can alter a clinician's sense of connection with others or lead her to lose touch with her sense of spirituality (Blanchard and Jones, 1997). Although hopefulness is a key component of good treatment, the therapist may experience a profound decrement in her sense of hope—for healing, for transformation, for triumph. Often the clinician's faith is shaken, and religion, nature, or other spiritual practices are no longer a comfort.

Another common example of ITW is exhaustion. For three years, Sara, a case manager in a mental health agency, worked with Anne, a thirty-five-year-old single white female diagnosed with major depressive disorder with psychotic features and a history of anorexia. They met twice each week and spent most of the time discussing the intensely painful feelings Anne experienced (rage, disappointment, and abandonment), her difficulties managing family relationships, and her plans for coping with these issues without self-injuring.

These sessions were emotionally draining for Sara, who, through supervision, developed a number of strategies to let go of the impact of the negativity and rage expressed by Anne. These strategies worked well until Anne's rage became focused on Sara over several months as Anne became increasingly agitated and psychotic. Anne now sought daily contact with Sara, requiring Sara to drop whatever she was doing to attend to her. Despite her demands for extra support and assistance, Anne insisted she was not getting "sick" and refused to consider a medication change or hospitalization. Anne became rageful and verbally abusive toward Sara on an increasingly personal level, cursing her and calling her names on a number of occasions. Sara began feeling defensive and angry, yet felt she needed to hide those feelings and instead be all the more patient and consistent in her work with Anne. Sara found her patience and energy for her other clients waning, and she had trouble sleeping well; she was dreaming about the conflict with Anne. She felt too tired to see friends. After helping Anne finally agree to be hospitalized and consider a change in medication to help her restabilize, Sara had to confront her personal sense of exhaustion and evaluate the toll that working with Anne, in the way in which she was, was having on her own health.

A clinician's ability to stay connected and grounded in a strong sense of self, even in the face of strong feelings, is weakened when his or her inner resources are depleted. Changes can occur in the clinician's ability to tolerate affect, maintain a positive sense of self, and maintain an inner sense of connection. How clinicians typically understand the behaviors of others and feel about significant events may even change during the course of their work. When faced with work that is consistently difficult and demanding, clinicians may come to feel off-balance, shaky, weepy, or angry, in addition to feeling chronically overwhelmed and exhausted. Under the worst of circumstances, clinicians may find that they are at risk for using some of the same self-destructive soothing strategies that plague their clients, engaging in the use of alcohol or drugs, gambling, or shopping excessively in order to relax, distract, or numb themselves (Pearlman and Saakvitne, 1995).

Factors That Heighten the Impact of Trauma Recovery Work

Several factors can intensify the impact of trauma work. A clinician working solely with trauma survivors, for example, may have more difficulty managing ITW than one who has a varied clientele or varied job responsibilities. It also becomes more difficult to manage the impact of trauma work when the policies and procedures of a clinic or mental health agency are in conflict with one another, in conflict with what the clinician feels is good practice, or in conflict with general trauma-informed principles.

Perhaps more than any other factor, trauma work is difficult when clinicians do not understand trauma dynamics. They may then report feeling that they and the consumer are at odds over goals or problem-solving approaches. When providers instead use trauma as a framework for understanding consumers' behaviors and attitudes, they can improve the collaboration with the consumer to develop jointly planned goals. With greater collaboration, the provider is more likely to feel empowered and energized in work, mitigating the effects of ITW.

Residential counselors were baffled and frustrated when a woman in urgent need of housing turned down a spacious apartment. In a traditional residential services program, the woman would have been labeled resistant and difficult, and the counselor might have become aggravated and responded by saying, "It's either that or the shelter. I know of no other available options right now." In contrast, the trauma-informed counselor explored the concerns of the woman, who then shared her fear about living across from a wooded area, which reminded her of the woods in which she had been raped years ago.

When clinicians consider that a trauma history may drive a woman's reticence to accept a recommendation, they are less likely to become angry and frustrated and engage in power struggles. When they understand and respect the consumer's valid concerns, they can more confidently advocate for the consumer to the rest of agency or the larger service system in order to gain support for finding an alternative solution.

An additional complication occurs when the clinician herself is a survivor of abuse and is dealing with her own abuse issues while attempting to deliver care and services to other trauma survivors. The effects of abuse alter most survivors' experiences of affect, body, memories, knowledge, and identity. These changes all relate to the self, the therapist's primary therapeutic tool. Trauma survivors who become therapists bring special strengths and skills to the work, as well as some unique issues to contend with as they consider what is necessary for their own self-care.

As a result of their experiences, survivor-clinicians have the potential to bring a unique understanding to their work with other trauma survivors. They may have a well-developed capacity to be attentive to the needs of others and may therefore be excellent caregivers. This very capacity can pose difficulties, however, for survivor-clinicians who may repeat a pattern of overextending oneself. For example, Cindy, a case manager, said, "Instead of encouraging consumers to use the agency on-call system, I found myself giving out my home telephone number. I thought I was the only one who truly understood and could be of comfort to the women I worked with."

Another challenge for survivor-clinicians is to recognize abuse issues accurately and consistently in the consumer. To defend against her own pain, the survivor-clinician may deny signs of abuse she sees in others. A further complication occurs when the survivor-clinician is not aware of her own abuse history. Under these circumstances, she may defend against the pain that consumers experience and have trouble listening to and believing what they have to say.

But even if she is aware of her own history, a survivor-clinician may unconsciously expect consumers to follow the same path of recovery that she did. Monica, a group therapist, expected and pulled for group members to be angry at their perpetrators. It took the feedback of her cotherapist for her to realize that she was acting on how she felt about her own abuser. Monica realized she was doing her own work in the group and was using the group to validate her own experience. She eventually became more aware that she needed to address her own issues apart from those of the consumers she served.

Along with other treatment providers, the survivor-clinician may seek therapy to work out issues of trust, control, boundaries, safety, and self-esteem in order to know her limitations and be more available to consumers. Someone whose boundaries have been consistently violated may find it difficult to determine and maintain healthy boundaries. Furthermore, self-care may be a new concept to the survivor-clinician. By understanding how to care better for herself, she will not only learn new skills and feel better, but she will have more energy and more options to offer the consumers with whom she works.

Solutions: Reducing the Impact of Trauma Recovery Work on Clinicians

Agencies as systems of care and clinicians as individuals can work to reduce ITW. Traditionally, clinicians have not been given permission to explore how they are affected by trauma work. Providers must be able to speak openly about their negative feelings about their work. Talking with other professionals counteracts isolation, restores connection, provides reality testing, and normalizes responses (Pearlman and Saakvitne, 1995).

In a trauma-informed system, agencies need first to acknowledge ITW and to grant that it is inevitable to some degree. As agencies normalize the response to ITW, clinicians are permitted to examine ITW without shame, blame, or the assumption of pathology. Agencies can then begin to minimize ITW by training all staff in trauma-informed practices. When clinicians receive training regarding trauma issues, learn how trauma presents in the lives of the consumers with whom they work, and learn different clinical strategies for working in a way that is sensitive to trauma issues, they will provide more effective services, avoid retraumatization of consumers, and decrease ITW.

In addition to providing professional education about trauma, an agency can validate the importance of clinician self-care in a number of ways.

Maurice, a child protective services worker, spent eight hours a day dealing with families, each telling a more horrifying story than the next. He had no opportunities for different types of work, such as teaching parenting skills classes or training or supervising other staff members. In addition, he seemed to get all the cases with young children who needed to be removed from their homes.

This child welfare agency, as well as any other type of social service agency, can support its clinicians by building an ongoing professional support system into its organizational structure. A trauma-informed agency will provide supervision and consultation for its clinical staff. The agency may use clinical teams so that not just one clinician, but a whole team shoulders responsibility for clinical work and coverage with consumers. This diffuses the intensity of individual relationships and models for both workers and consumers alike that everyone needs multiple people to create an effective support system.

Another way to diffuse the intensity of ITW is for agencies to give a variety of job responsibilities to each employee, balancing intense clinical work with training, writing, supervising, or participating in research. Agencies can support clinicians by varying the clinical work itself, providing the opportunity for a clinician to work with individuals, groups, couples, and families (Pearlman and Saakvitne, 1995). Agencies that have a narrow scope of work and therefore cannot offer their clinicians such variety in job responsibilities can consider creative alternatives to move to a more balanced clinical experience for employees.

Agencies can recognize the need for a safe, private, comfortable work environment that supports and respects not only the employees, but also the consumers. Agencies can also show their respect for clinicians' needs for self-care by providing reasonable benefits such as vacation time and adequate health plans.

The individual clinician can also take several actions to reduce ITW. Pearlman and Saakvitne (1995) discuss the concept of awareness: awareness of oneself, one's needs, and one's limits and resources. This awareness is necessary in order to develop personally relevant strategies for working with consumers and for self-care. In work, clinicians can increase their awareness of their own limits and boundaries and thereby prioritize the setting of clear boundaries with consumers. It is important for workers to know that it is not only appropriate but also imperative to set clear limits with consumers in the service of modeling respectful boundaries as well as taking care of themselves.

Marge, a woman with schizophrenia and an addiction to crack cocaine, regularly vented her frustrations about repeated housing evictions (subsequent to drug use in the house) to her case manager, Elena. When she escalated by screaming, cursing, and blaming Elena for her lack of housing, Elena immediately ended the meeting and told Marge, "It's not okay for you to yell at me and curse me out; let's try this again next week."

Elena set her own limits and held Marge responsible for her behavior. This limit empowered them both: Elena valued herself enough to prevent others from using her as a doormat, and Marge experienced herself as an adult who can be in control of her behavior.

To reduce ITW, clinicians can apply the practice of self-awareness within both the work environment and personal life. Consulting an individual therapist and building a rich social, recreational, or spiritual life can all serve to balance the stress of working with survivors of trauma.

Jackie, an addictions counselor, remarked, "When I started practicing yoga, I found I was able to let go of work stress so much that I had much more energy for family and friends. Yoga rejuvenates me in a way that television or a glass of wine never did."

Rest, play, and a variety of replenishing activities can serve to counterbalance the personal depletion brought on by doing trauma recovery work with a number of consumers.

The development of strategies for self-care is important so that clinicians can remain available to consumers, colleagues, and friends. These strategies counter loss of meaning and hope, loss of connection, and loss of awareness.

Conclusion

Care of the clinician should receive the same attention given to care of consumers. It is clinicians' responsibility to take care of themselves and become aware of their reactions in order to provide a safe emotional environment in which consumers can do their work. Furthermore, as clinicians model the importance of self-care, consumers learn to apply the same care to themselves. As agencies validate ITW and subsequently the need for clinician self-care, they create an atmosphere of empowerment, which is likely to foster greater staff satisfaction, less staff turnover, and the provision of more effective services for consumers.

References

Blanchard, E. A., and Jones, M. "Care of Clinicians Doing Trauma Work." In M. Harris and C. Landis (eds.), *Sexual Abuse in the Lives of Women Diagnosed with Serious Mental Illness.* Amsterdam: Harwood Academic Publishers, 1997.

Pearlman, L. A., and Saakvitne, K. W. *Trauma and the Therapist: Countertransference and Vicarious Traumatization in Psychotherapy with Incest Survivors.* New York: Norton, 1995.

ELLEN ARLEDGE is a clinical supervisor at Community Connections in Washington, D.C.

REBECCA WOLFSON is the clinical and training coordinator at the National Capital Center for Trauma Recovery and Empowerment at Community Connections.

INDEX

Absence of all feeling, 61
Access issues, 84
Addictions: culture of, 62–63; family histories of violence and, 60; to manage abuse impact, 60–62; sexual/physical abuse as risk factor for, 59
Addictions services: elements of trauma-informed, 63–73; integrating trauma and, 57–59; understanding links of trauma and, 59–63
Administration. *See* Staff members
Advance directives for housing, 53
Amaro, H., 62
American Psychiatric Association, 10, 28
Americans With Disabilities Act (1990), 5, 83
Anger/rage, 61
Anxiety, 61
Arledge, E., 91, 98
Assertiveness skills, 67
Assessment. *See* Trauma-informed assessment

Barbara's story, 81
Bebout, R. R., 47, 55
Berman, K., 63
Blanchard, E. A., 92
Bloom, S., 42
Boundary issues: group living and, 49–50; inpatient services and, 38–39; limit setting/assertiveness skills and, 67; trauma-informed approach to, 52–53
Brett, E., 27
Bryer, J., 3
Burnout, 91

Cabral, H., 62
Campbell, J. 84
Carling, P. J., 52
Carmen, E., 9, 44
Case management: authority/responsibility issues in, 77–78; clinical vs. everyday language used in, 79; management vs. empowerment in, 75–76; power/control issues in, 75–77; problems/disabilities vs. strengths in, 76–77; stabilization vs. growth/change goals of, 78–79; trauma-

informed service system, 79–83. *See also* Staff members
CASPAR (Consumer Action and Support Plan), 80
Center for Mental Health Services, 5
Center for Substance Abuse Prevention, 5
Center for Substance Abuse Treatment, 5
Chris's story, 79
Clients: avoiding retraumatizing, 44; using clinical vs. everyday language with, 79; collaborative housing decision making by, 54; empowerment of, 75–76, 78; housing arena and, 47–55; trauma-informed inpatient services for, 33–45; trauma-informed system and understanding of, 12–15; universal screening of, 6–7, 25; Wellness Recovery Action Plan for, 33–34, 43. *See also* Consumer-survivors
Clinical language, 79
Clinician self-care: importance of, 91–92; reducing ITW (impact of trauma) for, 95–97. *See also* Staff members
"Comfort card," 53
Communication skills, 68
Community Connections (Washington, D. C.), 6, 8–9, 21, 43, 62, 80
Compassion fatigue, 91
Complex PTDS, 27–28
Confrontation, 72
Consumer-survivor involvement: barriers to, 84–85; benefits of, 84; future development of, 89; recommended strategies for, 85–88
Consumer-survivor strategic plan, 86
Consumer-survivors: approaches to relationship with, 18–20; approaches to services for, 15–18; approaches to understanding, 12–15; avoiding retraumatizing of, 44, 51–52; coping strategies/new understanding by, 14–15, 30; failure to report trauma by, 23; role in trauma-informed systems by, 83–89; self-soothing behavior by, 41–42, 49, 53, 66–67; traditional service relationship with, 18–19; trauma-informed inpatient services for, 35–44; trauma-related

behaviors manifested by, 48–51; triggers/stressors of, 29–30, 40–41; Wellness Recovery Action Plan for, 33–34, 43. *See also* Clients; Trauma; Trauma screening
Contraindicated approaches, 71–72
Copeland, M. E., 33, 34
Coping strategies: identifying survivor, 30; during physical/sexual abuse, 14–15
Countertransference, 91
Criterion A1 trauma, 28
Criterion A2 trauma, 28

Darlene's story, 80
Deegan, P. E., 84, 85
Deescalation strategies, 39
Deficits in self-soothing, 53
Depression, 61
Desires/needs expression, 67–68
Devaluation language, 85
Disclosure issues, 84–85
Disconnection, 62
Disorders of Extreme Stress Not Otherwise Specified, 28
Dissociation coping strategy, 15
Drabble, L., 57
Dutton, M. A., 52, 62

Eating disorders, 50
Educational/vocational services, 69
Elaine's story, 79–80
Emotional safety assurances, 39–42
Empowerment: allocation of resources and, 78; limiting ITW through, 96–97; staff management vs., 75–76
Evans, K., 57, 59
Excessive anger/rage, 61
Expert intervention, 77–78
Extreme behaviors, 50

Fallot, R. D., 3, 22, 23, 31, 33, 37, 46, 57, 73
Finkelstein, N., 59, 63, 69
Fisher, D. B., 84, 85
Foa, E. B., 27
Freed, L., 62
Freeman, D. W., 37, 75, 82

Gamble, S., 7
Goodman, L. A., 52, 62
Harris, M., 3, 22, 23, 31, 33, 46, 52, 57, 62, 73
Health care issues, 71
Herman, J., 28, 66

Higher power, 72
Homelessness trauma, 52
Honest labeling skills, 68
Hospitalization alternatives, 33–35
Housing arena: avoiding retraumatization in, 51–52; collaborative decision making in, 54; controversies surrounding, 47–48; single-sex, 54; trauma-informed addictions program and, 70; trauma-informed approach to, 52–55; trauma-related behaviors manifested in, 48–51
Housing rules/expectations statement, 54

"Informed about trauma," 4. *See also* Trauma-informed service system
Inner turmoil/pain, 61
Inpatient services. *See* Trauma-informed inpatient services
Intrusive monitoring, 72
Isolation, 62
ITW (impact of trauma): described, 92–93; factors which heighten, 94–95; reducing impact of, 95–97. *See also* Staff members

Jennings, A., 9, 44
John's story, 77
Johnstone, L., 39
Jones, M., 92
Jordan, J., 65
Julie's story, 76

Kasl, C. D., 72
Keane, T. M., 27
Kearns, M., 69
Kennedy, C., 69
Kisthardt, W., 84
Krol, P., 3

Language: clinical vs. everyday, 79; devaluation, 85
Lazzaro, C., 39
Legal services, 70–71
Life skills, 70
Linehan, M., 35, 41

McCabe, S., 84, 86
McNasser, G., 39
Male/female inpatient separation, 37–38
Measuring progress strategies, 86
Miller, J., 3
Money management, 81–82

Monitoring progress strategies, 86
Moral inventories, 72
Mutuality, 68–69

Najavits, L., 3
National Association of State Mental Health Program Directors, 6
Needs/desires expression, 67–68
Nelson, B., 3

Pain/inner turmoil, 61
Parallel treatment model, 57–58
Parenting skills, 69–70
Passivity, 61
Paula's story, 81–82
Pearlman, L. A., 7, 91, 92, 93, 95, 96
Perception skills, 68
Physical abuse: as addiction risk factor, 59; assessment of, 28–30; coping strategies during, 14–15; example of cycle of, 14–15; in mental health housing, 51–52; response to inpatient accusations of, 42; substance abuse to manage impact of, 60–62; trauma-specific services to treat, 4–5; understanding trauma of, 10–12. See also Trauma
Physical safety assurances, 36–39
Policy reviews, 86–88
Power: abusive relationships/distribution of, 78; case management issues of control vs., 75–77; survivor protests regarding abuse of staff, 78–79
Prescott, L., 83, 89
Primum non nocere (do no harm), 10
Privacy needs: group living and, 49–50; inpatient services and, 38–39; trauma-informed approach to, 52–53
Proactive planning, 86
Psychoeducation, 77–78
PTSD (posttraumatic stress disorder): assessment of, 27–28; identifying, 24

Rage/anger, 61
Rapp, C. A., 84
Reciprocity, 68–69
Relationships: appreciating mutuality/reciprocity in, 68–69; approaches to service, 18–20; power distribution in abusive, 78; women and support through, 65
Resource allocation, 78
Retraumatization: avoiding inpatient, 44; avoiding mental health housing, 51–52

RICH guidelines, 7–8
Risking Connection (Saakvitne, Gamble, Pearlman, and Tabor Lev), 7
Root, M.P.P., 59

Saakvitne, K. W., 7, 91, 92, 93, 95, 96
Safety issues: consumer-survivor involvement and, 84–85; in housing arena, 70; during inpatient services, 36–42
Sanctuary, 42. See also Trauma-informed inpatient services
Screening. See Trauma-informed screening
Self-esteem skills, 67
Self-knowledge skills, 66
Self-regulation skills, 66
Self-soothing behavior: adaptive, 53; crossover skills for, 66–67; deficits in, 49; identifying and developing, 41–42
Self-trust skills, 67
Sequential treatment model, 57–59
Service relationship: traditional approach to, 18–19; trauma-informed approach to, 19–20
Setting limits, 67
Sexual abuse: as addiction risk factor, 59; assessment of, 28–30; dissociation as form of coping during, 15; during inpatient treatment, 37–38; in mental health housing, 51–52; response to inpatient accusations of, 42; substance abuse to manage impact of, 60–62; trauma-specific services to treat, 4–5; understanding trauma of, 10–12. See also Trauma
Sexual adjustment patterns, 50–51
Sexual numbing, 61–62
Shaming techniques, 71
Shera, W., 84
Single-sex housing, 54
Sleep disturbances, 48
Soliday, S., 44
Stabilization goals, 78–79
Staff members: abuse of power by, 78–79; availability of same-gender inpatient, 37; commitment to trauma-informed services by, 5–6; hiring trauma-informed, 8–9; ITW (impact of trauma) on, 92–97; survivor-clinicians as, 94–95; training in safe deescalation strategies, 39; training/education of trauma-informed, 7–8; trauma-informed approach to housing and, 53–54. See also Case management

Stein, J., 3
Stigma issues, 84–85
Stressors/triggers, 29–30, 40–41
Substance abuse. *See* Addictions
Suicidality, 62
Sullivan, J. M., 57, 59
Survivor-clinicians, 94–95
Sustainability, 86

Tabor Lev, B., 7
Thomas, K., 69
Time-out space, 38
Traditional approach. *See* Trauma service system
Training/education development, 7–8
Trauma: assessment of, 25–30; associated with homelessness/residential instability, 52; Criterion A1 and A2, 28; failure of survivors to report, 23; identifying current triggers/stressors of, 29–30, 40–41; integrating addictions services and, 57–59; screening of client, 6–7, 24–25; symptoms of, 61–62; traditional approach to understanding, 10–11; trauma-informed approach to understanding, 11–12; trauma-specific services treatment of, 4–5. *See also* Consumer-survivors; Physical abuse; Sexual abuse
Trauma histories/impact, 28–30
Trauma screening: defining, 24; techniques for effective, 24–25; universal, 6–7, 25. *See also* Consumer-survivors
Trauma service system: current focus of typical, 3–4; trauma-informed compared to, 4–5; understanding consumer survivor using, 12–13; understanding relationship with consumers, 18–20; understanding services using, 15–16; understanding trauma using, 10–11. *See also* Trauma-informed service system
Trauma survivors. *See* Consumer-survivors
Trauma symptoms: addiction to cope with, 61–62; skills building vs. management of, 77
Trauma-addictions integrated model: on addictions to manage abuse impact, 60–62; on family histories of violence, 60; parallel and sequential options of, 57–59; prevalence data in, 59; understanding links in, 59–63
Trauma-informed addictions program: avoiding contraindicated approaches

in, 71–72; building crossover skills during, 66–69; establishing milieu of, 64–66; including ancillary services in, 69–71; teaching integrative explanations in, 63–64
Trauma-informed approach: benefits of, 4–5; to housing, 52–55; to inpatient services, 33–42; understanding consumer survivor using, 13–15; understanding service relationship using, 19–20; understanding services using, 15–18; understanding trauma using, 11–12; universal trauma screening in, 6–7, 25. *See also* Trauma-informed service system
Trauma-informed assessment: described, 25; to housing, 52; as process, 25–26; of PTSD and Complex PTSD, 27–28; of trauma histories/impact, 28–30; of trauma and related diagnoses, 26–27
Trauma-informed case management: crisis planning/response in, 80–81; money management in, 81–82; treatment planning vs. service contracts in, 79–80. *See also* Case management
Trauma-informed housing approach, 52–54. *See also* Housing arena
Trauma-informed inpatient services: accusations of abuse during, 42; alternatives to, 33–35; avoiding retraumatizing practices during, 44; designing ideal unit for, 42–44; ensuring emotional safety during, 39–42; ensuring physical safety during, 36–39; overview of, 35–36
Trauma-informed screening: techniques for effective, 24–25; universal, 6–7, 25
Trauma-informed service system: benefits of using, 4–5; case management in, 75–82; consumer-survivor role in, 83–89; inpatient, 33–45; principles/philosophy of, 10–20; requirements for creating, 5–10; screening and assessment in, 23–30. *See also* Trauma service system; Trauma-informed approach
Trauma-informed service system principles/philosophy: on understanding of consumer-survivor, 12–15; on understanding service relationship, 18–20; on understanding services, 15–18; on understanding trauma, 10–12
Trauma-informed service system requirements: administrative commitment to

change as, 5–6; hiring practices of, 8–9; review of policies/ procedures as, 9–10; training/education as, 7–8; universal screening as, 6–7
Trauma-related behaviors: eating disorders/extreme behavior/sexual adjustment patterns as, 50–51; privacy needs/boundary issues as, 38–39, 49–50; self-soothing deficits as, 49; sleep disturbances as, 48
Trauma-specific services, 4–5
Triggers/stressors, 29–30, 40–41

Universal screening, 6–7, 25
Unzicker, R. E., 84, 86

van der Kolk, B. A., 27, 28
Van Tosh, L., 84
Vicarious traumatization, 91
Visalli, H., 39
Vocational/educational services, 69

Wallen, J., 63
Weathers, F. W., 27
Wellness Recovery Action Plan, 33–34, 43
"What Is Trauma?" (Community Connections presentation), 7
Wile, J., 36
Wolfson, R., 91, 98
Women: assessing trauma of sexually abused, 28–30; dissociation by sexually abused, 15; sleep disturbances of sexually abused, 48; support through relationships by, 65; trading sex for drugs, 63; trauma-informed addictions program for, 63–73; trauma-informed inpatient issues of, 36–38. See also Consumer-survivors
"Women grow in connection" concept, 65
Women Speak Out video (Community Connections), 8, 43

Zuckerman, B., 62

Back Issue/Subscription Order Form

Copy or detach and send to:
Jossey-Bass, 350 Sansome Street, San Francisco CA 94104-1342

Call or fax toll free!
Phone 888-378-2537 6AM-5PM PST; Fax 800-605-2665

Back issues: Please send me the following issues at $25 each.
(Important: please include series initials and issue number, such as MHS90.)

1. MHS   _____

_____

$ _____ Total for single issues

$ _____ Shipping charges (for single issues **only;** subscriptions are exempt
from shipping charges): Up to $30, add $5^{50} • $30^{01}–$50, add $6^{50}
$50^{01}–$75, add $8 • $75^{01}–$100, add $10 • $100^{01}–$150, add $12
Over $150, call for shipping charge

Subscriptions   Please ❏ start   ❏ renew my subscription to *New Directions for
Mental Health Services* for the year ___ at the following rate:

	Individual	Institutional
U.S.:	❏ Individual $66	❏ Institutional $121
Canada:	❏ Individual $66	❏ Institutional $161
All others:	❏ Individual $90	❏ Institutional $195

$ _____ Total single issues and subscriptions (Add appropriate sales tax for
your state for single issue orders. No sales tax for U.S. subscriptions.
Canadian residents, add GST for subscriptions.)

❏ Payment enclosed (U.S. check or money order only)

❏ VISA, MC, AmEx, Discover Card #_____ Exp. date_____

Signature _____ Day phone _____

❏ Bill me (U.S. institutional orders only. Purchase order required.)

Purchase order #_____

Federal Tax ID 135593032   GST 89102-8052

Name _____

Address _____

_____

Phone_____ E-mail _____

For more information about Jossey-Bass, visit our Web site at:
www.josseybass.com   **PRIORITY CODE = ND1**

OTHER TITLES AVAILABLE IN THE NEW DIRECTIONS FOR MENTAL HEALTH
SERVICES SERIES
H. Richard Lamb, Editor-in-Chief

MHS88   The Role of Organized Psychology in Treatment of the Seriously Mentally Ill,
        Frederick J. Frese, III
MHS87   What Mental Health Practitioners Need to Know About HIV and AIDS,
        Francine Cournos, Marshall Forstein
MHS86   Psychiatric Aspects of Violence: Issues in Prevention and Treatment, Carl C.
        Bell
MHS85   What the Oregon Health Plan Can Teach Us About Managed Mental Health
        Care, Rupert R. Goetz, Bentson H. McFarland, Kathryn V. Ross
MHS84   The Role of the State Hospital in the Twenty-First Century, William D.
        Spaulding
MHS83   Speculative Innovations for Helping People with Serious Mental Illness,
        Mona Wasow
MHS82   New Developments in Emergency Psychiatry, Glenn W. Currier
MHS81   Advancing Mental Health and Primary Care Collaboration in the Public
        Sector, Rupert R. Goetz, David A. Pollack, David L. Cutler
MHS80   Spirituality and Religion in Recovery from Mental Illness, Roger D. Fallot
MHS79   Building Teams and Programs for Effective Psychiatric Rehabilitation,
        Patrick W. Corrigan, Daniel W. Giffort
MHS78   Managed Behavioral Healthcare, David Mechanic
MHS77   Families Coping with Mental Illness, Harriet P. Lefley
MHS76   Developments in Geriatric Psychiatry, Lon S. Schneider
MHS75   Can Mandatory Treatment Be Therapeutic?, Mark R. Munetz
MHS74   The Successful Diffusion of Innovative Program Approaches, Ellen Jane
        Hollingsworth
MHS73   Improving Psychiatric Treatment in an Era of Managed Care, David Mechanic
MHS72   Managed Care, the Private Sector, and Medicaid Mental Health and
        Substance Abuse Services, Miles F. Shore
MHS71   Using Client Outcomes Information to Improve Mental Health and
        Substance Abuse Treatment, Donald M. Steinwachs, Laurie M. Flynn, Grayson
        S. Norquist, Elizabeth A. Skinner
MHS70   Dual Diagnosis of Major Mental Illness and Substance Abuse, Volume 2:
        Recent Research and Clinical Implications, Robert E. Drake, Kim T. Mueser
MHS69   Emerging Issues in Forensic Psychiatry: From the Clinic to the Courthouse,
        Elissa P. Benedek
MHS68   A Pragmatic Approach to Psychiatric Rehabilitation: Lessons from Chicago's
        Threshold Program, Jerry Dincin
MHS67   The Growth and Specialization of Emergency Psychiatry, Michael H. Allen
MHS66   Maturing Mental Health Systems: New Challenges and Opportunities,
        Leonard I. Stein, Ellen Jane Hollingsworth
MHS65   Clinical Studies in Case Management, Joel Kanter
MHS64   Assessing and Treating Victims of Violence, John Briere
MHS62   Family Interventions in Mental Illness, Agnes B. Hatfield
MHS59   Managed Mental Health Care, William Goldman, Saul Feldman
MHS56   Innovative Community Mental Health Programs, Leonard I. Stein
MHS54   Neurobiological Disorders in Children and Adolescents, Enid Peschel,
        Richard Peschel, Carol W. Howe, James W. Howe
MHS52   Psychiatric Outreach to the Mentally Ill, Neal L. Cohen
MHS51   Treating Victims of Child Sexual Abuse, John Briere
MHS50   Dual Diagnosis of Major Mental Illness and Substance Disorder, Kenneth
        Minkoff, Robert Drake

8423566R0

Made in the USA
Lexington, KY
02 February 2011